ANXIETY
TREATMENT TECHNIQUES THAT REALLY WORK

Practical exercises, handouts and worksheets for therapists

by
Stanley E. Hibbs, PhD

PESI
Publishing
& Media
www.PESI.com

Copyright © 2013 by Stanley E. Hibbs
Published by
PESI Publishing and Media
PESI, Inc.
3839 White Ave
Eau Claire, WI 54703

Printed in the United States of America

Cover Design: Matt Pabich
Edited by: Marietta Whittlesey & Bookmasters
Page Design: Bookmasters

ISBN: 978-1-93612-844-0

Library of Congress Cataloging-in-Publication Data

Hibbs, Stanley.
  Anxiety : treatment techniques that really work / by Stanley Hibbs, Ph.D.
    pages cm
  ISBN-13: 978-1-936128-44-0 (pbk.)
  ISBN-10: 1-936128-44-6 (pbk.)
  1. Anxiety--Treatment. 2. Anxiety disorders--Treatment. I. Title.
  RC531.H53 2013
  616.85'22--dc23
                          2013011810

Table of Contents

About the Author

A passion for treating anxiety has focused Stanley Hibbs, Ph.D. on a mission ... that no one needs to suffer with anxiety disorders. Over his 30 year career, Stan has successfully treated thousands of clients with anxiety, using his easy-to-understand explanations and techniques. Dr. Hibbs is the author of two other self-help books, *Anxiety Gone: The Three C's of Anxiety Recovery* and *Consider It Done: Ten Prescriptions for Finishing What You Start.*

A clinical psychologist, Dr. Hibbs maintains a robust private practice in Atlanta, GA. In addition, he regularly presents his highly acclaimed seminar, "Anxiety: Treatments that Really Work," to mental health providers nationwide. Prior going into private practice, he worked at a community mental health center, a drug treatment program for teens, and taught at several universities. Dr. Hibbs was a regular guest on the daily radio show, "Marriage & Family Today."

For Suzanne, who brings out the best in me.

List of Client Handouts

LISTED BY CHAPTERS

Chapter One: Introduction

Since 2010, I have had the great pleasure of traveling the country presenting my seminar, "Anxiety: Treatments That Really Work," to thousands of mental health professionals. I have presented at least three day-long seminars per month during that time. I must confess that I experienced considerable ANXIETY when I first took on this new professional activity. However, I have an abiding conviction that I do not want anxiety to keep me from doing worthwhile things. So true to my beliefs, I confronted my fear, and I have been having the time of my life!

The response to these seminars has been more positive than I ever dreamt possible. I have been truly humbled by the kind feedback from so many professionals. Many have suggested that I write a workbook that essentially follows the format of my seminars. This workbook is my response to those suggestions.

TREATING ANXIETY DISORDERS: A GREAT CLINICAL SPECIALTY

If you are a mental health professional who is trying to find your professional niche, I would suggest that the treatment of anxiety disorders is one of the most exciting and rewarding clinical specialties that you can choose. There are three reasons why I feel this way.

First, there are so many people who need help. According to estimates published by the Anxiety Disorders Association of America, approximately 40 million Americans suffer from anxiety problems significant enough to be diagnosed as an anxiety disorder. It is the largest single category of psychiatric conditions. About one in every three Americans will suffer from an anxiety disorder at some time during their lives. Anyone who is skilled in the treatment of anxiety disorders will always be in great demand.

Second, the treatments that we have today are extremely effective, having a very high rate of success. Many problems lack solutions, but anxiety is not one of them. You will be gratified to see how many of your clients make major changes for the better.

The third reason that treatment of anxiety disorders is such a great specialty is the people! Many of the people who have come to see me are some of the nicest and most pleasant people you will ever meet. They enter therapy with many reservations and doubts but often leave with a level of confidence that they would not have thought possible. I admire them so much, and I learn from them just as much, if not more, as they learn from me.

WORKBOOK GOALS

I have four goals in this workbook. The first is to provide you with a toolbox of tips and techniques to help you be more effective in treating anxiety. I have provided 36 client handouts that you are free to copy and share with your clients.

My second goal is to share my simplified model of how I explain anxiety to my clients. Most clinicians have a good understanding of what anxiety is all about. However, I have been surprised at how little my clients understand about what is going on with them. Perhaps you have noticed that **highly anxious people are very anxious about being anxious**. They worry excessively about their anxiety. They often believe that something is terribly wrong with them because they feel the way that they do. Much of this "anxiety about anxiety" is due to a lack of knowledge. However, when you dissect anxiety into its three component parts (physiological, cognitive, behavioral) and explain to clients exactly what is going on, they often feel quite relieved and are more hopeful about therapy.

A third goal is to write in an everyday casual style. I want to speak to you as if you were attending one of my seminars. I know that we all have advanced degrees and are used to reading textbooks written in academic language and technical jargon. I used that style in writing my master's thesis and Ph.D. dissertation, but I would rather not do so now. We can all read and write in that style, but it often puts us to sleep. I would rather write something easy and perhaps even enjoyable to read.

Finally, I hope I can convey some of the passion that I feel for working with anxiety. It is a tragedy that so many people allow their lives to be unduly restricted by anxiety. They avoid social events. They won't go to the shopping mall or attend movies. They won't fly on airplanes, ride in elevators, or drive on bridges or overpasses. They worry endlessly about finances, health, careers, children, politics, or countless other issues, but feel paralyzed to take any practical steps to address their concerns. They miss out on career opportunities because they are afraid. They suffer loneliness because they are too afraid to pursue relationships that could enrich their lives. This is all such a waste! Some degree of anxiety is inevitable in life, but it doesn't have to keep us from having the rich full lives we would like to have.

VARIETIES OF ANXIETY DISORDERS

We will be addressing several different anxiety disorders in this workbook. Although there are some differences between these disorders, they have many of the same underlying features, so our approach to treatment is quite similar for each disorder. Here are the specific disorders to be discussed:

> Panic Disorder (with and without agoraphobia)
> Two phobias that are often variations of Panic Disorder:
> > Fear of Flying
> > Fear of Highway Driving
> Social Anxiety Disorder
> Generalized Anxiety Disorder (aka excessive worry)

As a trained clinician, you no doubt notice that I have omitted several disorders. For example, I do not include most specific phobias such as fear of heights, fear of animals, weather fears, etc. There are just too many of these to do them justice. However, these conditions can often be successfully treated using many of the principles described in this workbook.

I also have not included Post Traumatic Stress Disorder (PTSD), because I do not claim any specific expertise in this area and there are numerous treatment approaches that address these problems (e.g., Dialectical Behavior Therapy). Although PTSD has been traditionally categorized as an Anxiety Disorder, this was changed in the most recent Diagnostic and Statistical Manual of Psychiatric Disorders (DSM-5). PTSD is now listed in a separate category named Trauma and Stress Related Disorders, which also includes Acute Stress Disorder. However, even with this change, PTSD and Acute Stress Disorder have many of the features of the anxiety disorders, so many of the principles found in this workbook can be helpful for that population as well.

You will also note that I have not included Obsessive-Compulsive Disorder (OCD). OCD has also long been listed as an Anxiety Disorder but this was also changed in the DSM-5. It is now included in a separate category named OCD and Related Disorders. This category includes OCD, Hoarding Disorder, Body Dysmorphic Disorder, and Trichotillomania (hair pulling). Again, while OCD has many anxiety features, there is a specific treatment approach (Exposure and Response Prevention) that is very effective with this condition and well described in other treatment manuals.

Chapter Two:
Evidence-Based Treatment Approaches

There are a number of ways to treat anxiety. You can use medication, systematic desensitization, EDMR, psycho-dynamic therapy, humanistic-existential therapies, and others. Desensitization can be very helpful for specific phobias; EDMR seems to benefit those coping with trauma, and all the other "talk therapies" can be helpful with social anxiety and worry. All these approaches have their place with certain clients, and I do not want to suggest that there is only one way to treat a problem. That said, there are currently two different approaches to therapy that have a solid research base and are recognized as evidence-based treatments for anxiety. These are Cognitive-Behavioral Therapy (CBT) and Mindfulness-Based Therapies such as Acceptance and Commitment Therapy (ACT).

CBT has been around a long time. It is based on the idea that it is not the situation that determines how I feel; it is my thoughts about the situation that determine my response. It is our beliefs, interpretations, attributions, evaluations, and mental judgments that make us feel the way we feel. For example, it is Sunday afternoon and I am relaxing at home. Out of nowhere my wife asks me, "What are your plans for today?" My emotional reaction to that question will depend solely on how I interpret it. If my thought is "She has some chore for me that I don't want to do," I am likely to feel a mixture of annoyance and subtle guilt because I know I should probably be doing something productive. However, if my thought is, "Maybe she has something fun planned or she is just curious," then my feelings will be more positive. It might be that I'll have both thoughts, so my feelings will be mixed. In any case, it is ultimately how I interpret her question that determines how I feel.

As thinking about CBT has evolved in recent years, some experts in the field have advanced a new approach called Metacognitive Therapy. Although essentially an outgrowth of CBT, this approach focuses on a different aspect of our thinking. Whereas CBT focuses on the content of our thoughts (e.g., "She has a chore for me"), Metacognitive Therapy focuses on the process of thinking itself and our beliefs and attitudes about our thoughts (or our thoughts about our thoughts). For example, let's say that I have a lot of worries ("I might lose my job. I might lose my house. I might get very sick and die."). However, in addition to these worries, I am also **worried about my worry** (e.g., "If I keep worrying this way, it will drive me crazy."). Or perhaps I have the belief that "Maybe worrying about this will prevent it from happening." To practitioners of Metacognitive Therapy, helping clients challenge these metacognitive beliefs is a major goal of treatment.

In general, the major tenet of CBT and Metacognitive Therapy is that much of our misery and suffering is caused by how we think. Change your thinking, and you'll feel better.

On the other hand, the major tenet of ACT is that much of our suffering is caused by our tendency to resist and struggle against the normal thoughts and feelings that are a part of life.

For example, if I am starting my first day at a new job, it would be natural to have feelings of anxiety; maybe even a high level of anxiety. However, if I have the attitude that anxiety is "wrong," "weak," or "dangerous," then I will try to fight it; but this will only serve to increase the anxiety. If I can accept and embrace the anxiety and give myself permission to feel it, then it will not be so much of a problem.

To understand ACT, you need to understand three basic concepts: mindfulness, acceptance, and commitment.

Mindfulness: In the mental health arena, this concept has been very popular in the past decade or so. You no doubt see books on the subject as well as brochures for seminars. In the simplest terms, mindfulness is the ability to be fully aware of our experience—thoughts, feelings, and physical sensations—without becoming overly entangled or distressed by them. For example, as I write this sentence the thought "I'm never going to finish this book" has just crossed through my mind. In response to this thought, I am experiencing feelings of discouragement and anxiety. The ability to be mindful of these thoughts and feelings allows me to choose how to respond to them. I can follow them down a path of hopelessness and despair ("I **really** will never finish it"), self-criticism ("I shouldn't have such negative thoughts"), or self-acceptance ("These are normal thoughts and feelings that will pass").

Acceptance: Another basic tenet is that there is a natural flow of awareness of thoughts, feelings, and physical sensations that is constantly changing. What we think and feel in one moment will likely change the next moment. If we have a tendency to label our moment-to-moment experience as "bad," "wrong," or "dangerous," we will resist and struggle against them, which only adds to our unhappiness. It is better to be compassionate towards ourselves and accept our thoughts and feelings as they are. This concept is particularly useful in dealing with anxiety. Many people have decided that any level of anxiety is dangerous and unacceptable. So, if they begin to feel even the slightest bit of anxiety, they will say to themselves, "This is awful; I have to stop being so anxious." Of course, this only exacerbates the anxiety and makes it more of a problem. However, if they can accept and embrace anxiety as a normal human emotion and stop trying to fight it, it will be less of a problem. Even cognitive therapists such as David Burns use the term "acceptance paradox." They agree that the first step to dealing with an unpleasant emotion is to accept that it is there and not judge yourself for having it.

Commitment: Practitioners of ACT contend that it is a very behaviorally focused therapy. In the end, it is what we **do** that determines the quality of our lives. Since our momentary thoughts and feelings are constantly changing, we do not necessarily want them to govern the choices we make. Instead, we want to make choices based on the commitments we have made to ourselves and others and the core values upon which those commitments were made. In reality, we have almost no control over the thoughts and feelings that come our way, but we can control how we interpret them, and we can absolutely control the behavioral choices that we make.

In addition to CBT, Metacognitive Therapy, and ACT, we will be using Motivational Interviewing as a way to enhance client motivation and encourage them toward positive behavioral change. It is not a type of therapy but a way to keep clients engaged in the therapy process, no matter what other treatment approaches you might use. We will learn more about Motivational Interviewing in the next chapter.

Chapter Three:
Assessing and Enhancing Client Motivation

When I first started treating anxiety problems, I was so excited about these techniques that I would jump right in and start treatment. Given my enthusiasm, I was often taken aback by the client's reluctance. I should not have been surprised. People who struggle with anxiety are not particularly hopeful or optimistic. It is essential that we realize this fact and do all that we can to develop a solid relationship with the client before getting into the nuts and bolts of treatment. A first step is the get a clear idea of how anxiety is negatively impacting the client's life. How does it impact his or her emotional well-being? Social life? Career? Health? To help clients identify the cost of their anxiety, you are welcome to copy Handout 3-A.

HANDOUT 3-A
THE COST OF YOUR ANXIETY PROBLEM

Congratulations on your decision to address your problems with anxiety. To help you with this, take some time to think about how anxiety is negatively impacting various areas of your life. Circle any items that are relevant to you and include any others that you can think of.

Emotions: Worry, panic, depression, low self-esteem, hopelessness, frustration, anger, guilt.

What other emotions have you felt?

Health: Poor sleep, headaches, loss of appetite, stress eating, muscle tension, heart palpitations, sweating, stomach problems, fatigue.

What others have you experienced?

Vocational: Poor concentration on the job, absenteeism, passing up jobs/promotions due to anxiety.

What others have you experienced?

Social: Avoiding crowds, turning down invitations, excessive anxiety in social situations, loss of relationships.

What others have you experienced?

Family: Disrupted relationships with family members, criticism from family members because of your anxiety problems.

What others have you experienced?

Lifestyle: Anxiety can cause us to miss out on activities that we might enjoy. Do any of these apply to you? Travel, flying in airplanes, driving on highways, shopping malls, sporting events, movies/theaters.

What other worthwhile activities do you avoid because of anxiety?

THE PAYOFF LIST

Although reviewing the cost of a client's anxiety can be motivating, it can also make the client feel overwhelmed and too discouraged to take action. So, it is also important to spend significant time exploring what a client hopes to get from treatment. My approach is to ask the client to write a "payoff list." I encourage the client to be concrete, specific, and detailed in writing the payoffs. Sometimes we tend to be too vague in describing our goals. For example, a person might say that a goal is to "feel better." This is all well and good, but such a general description is not likely to motivate us when the going gets tough. A better-worded payoff might be "I have a positive outlook about life that I show by being friendlier to my friends and co-workers. This is allowing me to develop great relationships and I can involve myself in more social activities. I engage in at least one worthwhile social activity per week, such as attending the small group at church or going out for drinks with co-workers."

This kind of specific payoff does a lot to maintain motivation throughout therapy. People give up on things because they focus on the work and forget why they are doing the work. They are much more likely to stay the course if they keep their payoffs in front of them. Clients can use Handout 3-B to help them develop their payoff lists.

HANDOUT 3-B
YOUR PAYOFF LIST

Take some time to think about what you want to get from therapy. You will be more motivated to complete therapy if you have a clear picture of your goals. You are encouraged to develop a "payoff list." A payoff should be a specific, detailed, and emotionally charged description of what you hope to get from therapy. It is very important that you be specific and concrete. For example, if you want to lose weight you might say you want to "be healthier." That is fine for a start, but it's probably too vague to keep you on your diet/exercise plan when the going gets tough. However, imagine your payoff as "I can go on hikes, do yard work, and play tennis without losing my breath. I will live a long, healthy, and vibrant life until well into my 90s. I can attend the graduations and weddings of my children and grandchildren. I can play with my grandchildren." Can you see how this might be more motivating?

Use the form below to help you put together your payoffs. Use the questions to help guide your writing.

What negative feelings do you want to have less of? (e.g., worry, panic, etc.)

_____

_____

_____

_____

What positive feelings do you want more of? (e.g., calm, confident, relaxed, self-assured)

_____

_____

_____

_____

What behaviors do you want to be able to do? (e.g., travel, go to social events, ask the boss for a raise)

_____

_____

_____

_____

What will be the benefit of those behaviors? (e.g., If I get the raise, I will have $10,000 more income, which will allow me to put my child in private school.)

_____

_____

_____

Now write your payoffs below. Write them in the first-person, present tense, as if they were already true. Once you have developed your payoff list, post it somewhere you can review it often.

MOTIVATIONAL INTERVIEWING

Positive change is difficult, and we need to do all we can to encourage our clients to stay the course. One approach that is extremely helpful is Motivational Interviewing (MI). MI was developed by two psychologists, William R. Miller and Stephen Rollnick. They were primarily interested in addiction treatment. Traditionally the treatment of alcoholism and drug dependence has been very "in your face." Individuals are confronted with the facts of their drug use. If individuals resist this, they might be labeled as "in denial" and not ready to face their problems until they "hit bottom." This approach has helped a lot of people, so we cannot argue against its usefulness in many cases. However, Miller and Rollnick wondered if perhaps some of the people who had not "hit bottom" might be willing and able to pursue recovery if they were handled in a different way. MI was their creation, and research has demonstrated that programs that employ MI show an increase in the percentage of clients who engage in and complete therapy.

MI involves both specific techniques and an underlying spirit that honors the autonomy of the client. It is often described as "client centered" because the focus is on the client's own internal motivation as the source of change. However, it is also "directive" in that both client and therapist agree that the client wants and needs to make behavioral changes.

It is impossible to do justice to MI in this brief description. I can, however, describe the main idea behind MI. In MI we rethink the concept of "resistance" in psychotherapy. In the past, when a patient was stalled or was pushing back on an interpretation or suggestion, we would attribute it totally to the "defensiveness" of the client. In other words, it was the client's fault. The focus in MI is different. Instead of being "resistant" or "in denial," clients are seen as "normally ambivalent." Every individual will have mixed feelings about change. The alcoholic both wants to quit but also has great objections to quitting. Don't we all want to be thin and fit, but do any of us want to diet and exercise? This ambivalence is not pathological; it's normal, and we must be willing to affirm and honor the client's mixed feelings and motives.

Sometimes when we encourage clients to make positive changes, our efforts backfire and the client remains more steadfastly committed to not changing. This is because if you push on one side of the ambivalence, people tend to push back from the other side. We are all like this! If someone says to me, "You really need to start exercising," my reply might be, "Yes, but I just don't have the time."

I am sure you sometimes find yourself in a "Why don't you? Yes, but ..." wrestling match with your clients. Even after 30 years of experience, I still get into them. We might get annoyed with our clients for this, but it is really our fault. We need to honor and affirm the client's ambivalence.

Here is a good example of how and how not to do it. I have been working with Steve for several months. He has been taking about how much he needs a raise in his salary at work. His family is struggling financially. Plus, his performance reviews are excellent and he is way overdue for a raise. Trying to be encouraging, I might say:

"Steve, it sounds like you really need and deserve the raise. How would you feel about our working together to prepare you to talk to the boss?"

Steve's reply might be, "Oh, I don't think so. I am so intimidated by him; I just don't think I could do it."

Not taking no for an answer, I might say, "Steve, I understand how scary he is. Nevertheless, you have learned to be a lot more assertive in many situations. What if we applied some of the things we've learned from these other situations?"

"Those situations were a lot easier. This would be a lot harder. I'm just not ready."

Can you see what is happening? As the therapist, I have all the positive lines. Steve is responding with all the negative lines. Social psychologists say that we tend to believe what we hear ourselves say, so I am systematically discouraging Steve from asking for the raise.

It would be much better for me to acknowledge both sides of the ambivalence. A good response might be, "You are really intimidated by this guy and just don't feel ready to talk with him. In fact, you wonder if you'll ever be ready. And you know that you really need and deserve the raise." In MI, this is called a "double-sided reflection," because I have shown equal respect for both sides of his internal argument. You also will notice that I used the conjunction "and" instead of "but." This is because the two sides are not contradictory. They are both completely true statements.

If I show this equal respect for both sides, Steve is more likely to say something like "I wish I had the nerve." Steve is not making a commitment here. He just says he "wishes" he could. This is an example of what is called "change talk" in MI. Change talk is anything the client says that suggests some leaning toward or inclination toward change. It's not change itself; it's just talking about the possibility of change.

In MI, we talk about four types of change talk. The four types spell the acronym DARN.

> D stands for Desire, so we look for statements like "I wish," "I would like to," or "I want to."
>
> A stands for Ability, or statements that suggest that the client has some confidence that change might be possible. These include statements such as "I could," "I might be able to," or, as we say in the South, "I might could."
>
> R stands for Reasons, in which the client describes the possible benefits of change. For example, "I know it would really help my family if I could get that raise."
>
> N stands for Need and is illustrated by statements such as "I should," "I ought to," and "I need to."

When we hear change talk, we need to affirm it by reflecting it back to the client ("You would really love to be able to do this") or by asking questions to evoke more change talk ("Tell me some more about what the raise would mean to you," or "If you did have the nerve, how do you think you would do it?").

We don't want to be doing the change talk; our goal is to encourage the client to engage in change talk. When we do this, the client may eventually get to "commitment talk." Then, and only then, can we work with the client to develop a behavioral plan.

To illustrate the difference between change talk and commitment talk, I like to tell my seminar participants about my wedding day over 30 years ago. I am standing at the altar with my beautiful bride. The pastor asks me, "Stan, do you take Suzanne to be your lawfully wedded wife?" What if I had said "I'd like to," or "I should," or "It would be good if I did"? I probably wouldn't be married today, would I? However, if the pastor had been trained in MI, he might have saved the day by asking, "So you really think you should. Why do you think it would be a good idea?"

Often if the client is ambivalent about treatment, it is helpful to have the client lists the pros and cons of pursuing therapy and trying to change. I encourage my clients to use Handout 3-C to list their reasons to try therapy and their reasons for not trying it. Obviously, you are hoping that the client's reasons for change will outweigh the reasons not to change, but you must take a neutral stance. You do not take sides, but give clients the space to decide for themselves if the advantages outweigh the disadvantages.

In the spaces below list the advantages and disadvantages of seeking therapy to overcome your anxiety problems. To help you get started, some common reasons are listed. Mark the ones that are relevant to you and add any others that come to your mind. Your therapist can help you with this.

Reasons to seek therapy:

> It might work.
>
> I want a better life.
>
> My family will be proud.
>
> I'm sick of the way things are.
>
> I'm missing out on things I want to do.
>
> I'm tired of suffering so much.

List some more reasons below:

Reasons not to seek therapy:

> It might not work.
>
> It will make me feel anxious.
>
> It will cost time and money.
>
> I'm comfortable the way I am.
>
> It's not really so bad.
>
> I don't want to do the work.

List some more reasons below:

HELPING CLIENTS FOLLOW THROUGH WITH HOMEWORK: THE MOTIVATIONAL RULER

Most therapists understand that therapy is not a passive process. Success depends on clients' willingness to do "homework," or action steps that they will take between sessions. It might be something they do, something they write, something they read, or a conversation with someone. Homework in therapy is not like it was in school where you had no choice in what homework was assigned. The process for developing homework is a collaborative process. Therapists can suggest ideas for homework, but ultimately it will be up to the client to decide what steps to take. It doesn't matter how small a step is, as long as it is in the direction the client wants to go.

Sometimes I refer to homework tasks as "experiments." That is, we are just going to try sometime and see what happens. This term reduces the pressure clients feel to "get it right." There is no "right" outcome. Whatever happens can be useful in moving therapy forward.

Even though homework completion is such a key component in therapy, many clients have great difficulty following through with what they have agreed to do. There is a wonderful tool from Motivational Interviewing that can help with that. It is called The Motivational Ruler.

Here is how it works: After the client has developed an action step, you ask, "To help you be successful at this, would it be OK if I asked you a few questions?" Clients invariably agree to this. There are four questions you can ask, although you do not necessarily have to ask all four questions. Choose the questions based on what would be most relevant to the client. Here are the four questions:

1. "On a scale of 1–10, 1 being very low, 10 being perfectly high, how willing are you to do this task?"   If you get an answer of 8 or above, you are in good shape, but if you get anything below that, you have some work to do. A powerful question to ask is, "Why is it higher than 1?" You word the question this way because you want to determine what level of willingness the client has. Asking "Why isn't it higher?" will only focus on the reasons not to do it. After this discussion, the client either needs to be more willing or you need to modify or completely change the task so it is something that he or she is more willing to do.

2. "On a scale of 1–10, how important is it that you do this?"   Often clients will tell you that an action step is important even if they have a low level of willingness to do it. For example, clients will say that they know exposure practice is important but still have little willingness to do it. Again, if you get a response less than 8, you have some work to do.

3. "On a scale of 1–10, how confident are you that you can and will do this?"   It is not uncommon for clients to tell you that an action step is very important and they are willing to do it, but they doubt their ability to follow through when the time comes. When you get scores below 8, you might need to slice the task down into smaller steps, or come up with a completely different task. Again, you eventually want the client to respond with at least an 8.

4. "On a scale of 1–10, how ready are you to absolutely commit to this task?"   This is a crucial question because it lets clients know that homework is not busywork but an essential component of therapy. It's at this point where "change talk" becomes "commitment talk." Clients do not need to be ready for every step that they might need to make, but they need to be ready to take the next step, no matter how small it might be.

OVERCOMING EXCUSES

This next motivational technique should be reserved until after you have developed some rapport with your clients, they seem comfortable with you, and you feel like you can be a little light-hearted and playful with them. It addresses the all-too-human trait of making excuses for our behavior. I always introduce this topic by admitting that I am a terrible excuse maker and it is not shameful to make excuses. However, if we are to be successful in any endeavor, we need to be willing to identify and overcome excuses.

I begin by asking this question: "If at any point you decide not to do this, what excuses will you make?" Clients often laugh and maybe blush a bit, but I have never had a client who couldn't come up with at least three to five good excuses. I ask them to write down their first excuse and leave a few empty lines before writing their second, third, fourth, and so on excuse.

Then, for each excuse, we come up with a firm but gentle rebuttal. The rebuttal must begin with what is true about the excuse, but then identify ways to dispute it. Suppose, for example, that you have decided to start an exercise program tomorrow. You set your alarm clock to wake up 30 minutes earlier. However, after the alarm goes off you begin to waver in your commitment. What is the first excuse you might make? Maybe it would be, "I'm too tired." If so, write that down and skip a few lines. What is your second excuse? "I don't have enough time." OK, write that down and skip a few lines. What is the next excuse? "I'll start tomorrow." Write that down and so one until you have listed every possible excuse you can think of.

You should begin your rebuttals by acknowledging what is true about the excuse. So it would begin with "Yes, I am tired …" Then write the magical word "nevertheless," and finish the sentence. So your rebuttals might be:

"Yes, I'm tired. Nevertheless, I will get energy if I get up and get going."

"Yes, I don't have a lot of time. Nevertheless, I can use the time that I have."

"Yes, I could start tomorrow. Nevertheless, I will be so much ahead if I start today."

To help clients succeed in overcoming excuses, I have included Handout 3-D.

HANDOUT 3-D
OVERCOMING EXCUSES

(Or, "The dog didn't really eat my homework")

If there is one thing that is true of all human beings, it's that we sometimes make excuses for our behavior. We don't always do what we say we will, and excuses are the way we try to make it right; at least in our own minds. NEVERTHELESS, if we want to accomplish anything important in life, we must recognize and overcome our excuses. To help you work through your excuses, I have devised a fun activity which allows us to humorously confront and overcome them.

Step One: Identify the target behavior (e.g., starting an exercise program).

Step Two: Write down all the possible excuses you can think of for not engaging in the target behavior (e.g., "I am too tired." "I don't have time." "I'll start tomorrow." "I don't feel like it."). Skip some lines between each excuse, because you are going to write something under each one.

Step Three: Develop a firm but gentle rebuttal for each excuse. Each rebuttal should begin by acknowledging whatever is true about the excuse (e.g., "Yes, I'm tired."). Then you write down one of the most powerful words in the world, NEVERTHELESS. Then you complete the sentence.

Examples:

"Yes, I'm tired. Nevertheless, I will get energized if I get started."
"Yes, I do not have a lot of time. Nevertheless, I can use the time I have."
"Yes, I could start tomorrow. Nevertheless, I will be just that much ahead if I start today."
"Yes, I don't feel like it. Nevertheless, I want the results so I will be glad if I get started."

(Note: These are just examples. Write down the excuses and rebuttals that best fit your situation.)

Step Four: Write you rebuttal statements on an index card (or in your electronic device) and review them regularly.

I cannot overstate the importance of continuously monitoring clients' level of motivation and working with them to keep them engaged in the process. People give up on things because they lose sight of what they hope to gain. So when a client becomes discouraged, go back over their payoff lists to see if they are still willing to do the work to get what they want. With all this in mind, let us move on to the meat and potatoes of anxiety treatment.

Chapter Four: Anxiety Unpacked: The Three Components of Anxiety

I have often observed that people who struggle with severe anxiety problems are often very **anxious about being anxious**. That is, anxiety itself is the focus of much of their concerns. Their experiences with anxiety have left them with the idea that anxiety is a terrible, dangerous, and unbearable emotion that must be avoided at all costs. This motivates them to fight, resist, or suppress any semblance of anxious feelings. This rarely works and only serves to make the anxiety worse.

In addition, many anxiety sufferers criticize themselves for having anxiety. They believe that if they were just stronger, smarter, tougher, or had more faith, they wouldn't be having these awful feelings. Low self-esteem is often a collateral effect for these individuals.

Much of this anxiety about anxiety comes from lack of knowledge. Anxiety sufferers are bewildered and mystified by their anxiety and do not understand what is happening to them. However, if you give clients clear, direct, and concrete information about what is going on with them, their anxiety is often reduced and they will be more optimistic about treatment. To help clients better understand their anxiety, we divide it into its three components: (1) physiological, (2) cognitive, and (3) behavioral. For each component, we have a goal that we hope to achieve. I refer to these as "The Three C's of Anxiety Recovery": Calm the body, Correct your thinking, and Confront your fears.

The physiological component refers to all the physical sensations that often accompany anxiety: rapid heartbeat, difficulty breathing, perspiration, muscle tension, stomach distress, and many others. These sensations, which are often dreaded by clients, are actually the body's natural and helpful response to a perceived danger. Once clients understand what is going on, they do not fear what the body is doing. Even though these sensations are completely harmless, they are unpleasant, so we give clients time-tested methods to empower them to reduce these sensations if they so desire. This is the first C: Calm the body.

The cognitive component refers to the Automatic Negative Thoughts (ANTS) that accompany anxiety. When we are highly anxious, we are likely too focused on dangers and threats, while not noticing information that might be reassuring or encouraging. So much of good therapy for anxiety involves helping clients identify their ANTS and replace them with more positive cognitions. I refer to this as the second C: Correct your thinking.

Finally, the behavioral component refers to our tendency to avoid situations that might trigger anxiety. However, that is often not a very helpful strategy. Avoidance only serves to make us more fearful of the situation and may keep us from doing things that we might like to do. This is the third C: Confront your fears.

All good anxiety treatment involves the Three C's to some degree. Let's review the Three C's in depth and then explore how to use them to treat specific anxiety disorders.

Chapter Five: The Physiological Component

When we are in the midst of an episode of intense anxiety or panic, our bodies react in ways that may alarm us. Physical sensations can include rapid heartbeat, difficulty breathing, perspiration, tingling sensations in the arms and legs, feeling dizzy or faint, muscle tension, and stomach distress. Use Handout 5-A to help clients identify their unique patterns of physical sensations.

Here are some physical symptoms commonly associated with anxiety and panic. Which do you have?

Symptoms often seen in panic attacks:

> Rapid heartbeat
>
> Difficulty breathing or feeling like you can't get enough air
>
> Perspiration
>
> Jitteriness
>
> Numbness or tingling in arms, hands, and/or feet
>
> Feeling light-headed, dizzy, or like you're going to faint
>
> Stomach distress including nausea or diarrhea

What others do you have?

These symptoms are more often associated with longer-term and less intense anxiety and worry:

> Irritability or feeling "on edge"
>
> Headaches
>
> Sleep problems

What others do you have?

It is helpful for clients to learn that there is one legitimate purpose for fear: to save our lives if we are in literal physical danger. I tell my clients that the human body is a wonderful piece of machinery, but it is woefully out of date. It is still wired for life in the wild.

Science has taught us that for the bulk of human history, we lived in a natural environment in which our survival often was based on the ability to escape predatory animals or other humans bent on our destruction. We needed a way to respond quickly and efficiently to danger. So through evolution, we developed an emergency response system. This system is largely mediated in the lower, sub-cortical regions of the brain. It is also influenced by the endocrine system through hormones such as adrenalin. You and I are alive today largely because our ancestors had this system.

To illustrate, I love to tell clients about Mr. Caveman going for a walk (see Handout 5-B). Suddenly, he sees a tiger. Even before the language area of the brain has registered the word "tiger," the emergency response system has jumped into action. It senses danger and prepares our Caveman to escape. To run away, he must move his large muscle groups, such as the arms and legs. This movement requires fuel, which is supplied by the blood. So, the emergency system says to the heart "beat fast and hard." This is why "heart palpitations" are a common symptom of panic attacks. Here is a common dialogue that I might have with a client:

Me:	"Do you know why your heart races during panic attacks?"
Client:	"Because I'm afraid."
Me:	"Yes, but of all the things your body could be doing, why does it choose to do that?"
Client:	"It must have something to do with fight or flight."
Me:	"That's right, but why? Again, of all the things your body could do, why do that?"
Client:	"I don't know."

This is where I talk to them about Mr. Caveman and make a very important point: **This reaction is actually a good thing. It is exactly what you would want your body to do in a real emergency.**

Likewise, all of this burning of fuel requires oxygen, so the emergency response system says to the lungs "breathe fast." That explains why people often feel like they have lost control of their breathing, or they can't catch their breath, or somehow they are not getting enough air. Again, even though this sensation is unpleasant, it is the body's way of preparing you to escape and thus save your life.

All of this burning of energy will create heat, so the emergency system says to the sweat glands "sweat!" That is why we perspire when we're anxious. It's a good thing.

The blood flows from the brain because there is no use in pondering the truths of the universe if you're running for your life. This may create the feeling of light-headedness, dizziness, or feeling like you're going to faint. Again, this is a natural response and would save your life in real danger.

The capillary blood vessels in the skin might constrict. The purpose of this is to divert the blood to the large muscle groups where it is most needed. Plus, if Mr. Caveman is bitten by the tiger, he will bleed less if the blood is not near the surface. This can create the feeling of tingling or numbness in the extremities.

Certainly, the muscles will tense as you prepare to run (or perhaps fight if need be), so it is only natural that you would experience muscle tension or jitteriness.

Finally, blood will be diverted from the area around the digestive system and directed to the large muscle groups where it is really needed. After all, why digest your breakfast if you are about to be the tiger's breakfast? This creates nausea or digestive distress.

The problem is that for eons of human history, we have associated these physical sensations with danger and the need to escape. That is why people in the throes of a panic attack always feel that they have to get away from wherever they happen to be, even though there is no rational reason for doing so. **But this feeling of danger is a lie. You are not in any danger and there is no need to escape.**

A panic attack is a false alarm. The body is reacting to a danger that isn't there. Many of us have home security systems that go off by mistake. Likewise, we sometimes get these annoying buzzer sounds on TV or radio with the message, "This has been a test of the emergency response system. Had this been a real emergency, you would have been direct to …"

Thankfully, in our modern world, we do not need our emergency response system very often. However, we still have the system and sometimes it goes off when it isn't needed. It's just a mistake; that's all!

So here are some important facts to share with your clients:

1. These sensations are not harmful or dangerous in any way.

2. They are time limited. This makes sense because in the wild, emergencies were short-lived events. When you are running from a tiger, you will either make it to the cave or be dead pretty quickly, so there is no need for long-lasting states of arousal. Of course, we can keep the panic going by how we think about it, but if you do nothing a panic attack will subside in a few minutes.

3. The physical reactions of panic are very similar to what happens in your body during other states, including excitement, anger, and exercise. People ride on roller coasters in order to be excited and create the same sensations one has during a panic attack. You will note that people struggling with anxiety are often reluctant to do anything that will get them stirred up. Likewise, anxious people often do not like getting angry. And they often resist engaging in aerobic exercise, even though that is one of the best things for them to do.

You can use Handout 5-B to help educate clients on the truth about their physical sensations. Often this information is very helpful in lessening their fear of their bodies.

HANDOUT 5-B
UNDERSTANDING THE PHYSICAL SENSATION OF ANXIETY

(Or, Mr. Caveman goes for a walk)

During a panic attack, it is quite natural to believe that your body or mind has betrayed you. You are having a heart attack. You feel like you're dying. You believe that you must be losing control or going crazy.

However, your body is not betraying you. In fact, it is trying to help you, to protect you from a danger that isn't there.

The human body is a wonderful apparatus, but it is out of date. We are still wired for life in the wild. We each have an "emergency response system" that involves lower centers of the brain and the hormonal system. The function of this system is to save your life if you are in literal physical danger. We are alive today largely because our ancestors had this system.

So, let's imagine that Mr. Caveman is out for a walk when he comes across a tiger. Even before the language area of his brain has registered the word "tiger," his emergency system is getting him ready to run. To run, you have to move large muscle groups (legs, arms, etc.). This movement requires fuel, so it is essential that large amounts of blood be immediately delivered to these areas. To make this happen, the emergency system says to the heart, "We need blood. Pump fast and hard." That is why you experience a rapid heartbeat during a panic attack. So rather than being a bad thing, your heart is trying to do a good thing. You don't like the way it feels, but it's a good thing nonetheless.

To move large muscle groups, you have to get a lot of oxygen to the large muscle groups. So the system says, "We need air; breathe fast and shallow." This is why people often feel like they can't breathe. Again, the sensation might be unpleasant but it is actually a good response.

This burning of fuel will create heat, so the system says to the sweat glands, "Sweat!" Blood flows from the brain in order to get to the large muscle groups. This is why you might feel dizzy, light-headed, or like you might faint. Again, it feels bad, but it is a good thing!

Digestion stops because there is no need to digest your meat if you're going to be meat any second! This is why people experience stomach distress or nausea.

The small blood vessels on the surface of the skin constrict, so the blood will go deeper into the muscle tissue. This is why you might feel tingling or numbness in your hands and feet.

So all these response would save your life if confronted by a tiger; the problem is that there is no tiger. A panic attack is essentially a false alarm.

Here are some important facts to remember: (1) These reactions are normal and harmless. Nothing bad is happening to you. (2) These responses are time-limited; they don't last very long. We can keep them going by how we think about them, but if we do nothing they will go away. (3) These responses are similar to what happens when you're excited, when you're angry, and when you exercise.

You will be given some tools to help you reduce the intensity of these responses, but our ultimate goal will be for you to trust your body and be OK even if your body is not particularly calm at any point in time.

TECHNIQUES TO CALM THE BODY

Although we now understand that the physical symptoms of anxiety are not harmful, we would rather not feel them if we have a choice. Fortunately, we have some time-tested methods that can help reduce or eliminate these symptoms.

The first is **deep abdominal breathing**. We have known for a long time that deep breathing can help calm and relax the body. That is why pain clinics, childbirth classes, and yoga classes all make use of deep breathing. Most of the responses of the emergency response system are reflexes, and we have almost no control over them. However, we have a manual override with breathing because we can voluntarily slow it down and make it deeper. That in itself helps people feel more in control.

The key to deep breathing is to let the diaphragm drop and allow the breath to go all the way to the bottom of the lungs. You can imagine that your stomach is a balloon and you are blowing up the balloon with each inhale.

Unfortunately, many of us have forgotten how to breathe deeply. When asked to take a deep breath, many of us will suck in our stomachs. So, it takes some practice to master the technique. You can share Handout 5-C with clients to help them learn some deep-breathing techniques.

It is very important that clients practice deep breathing often. I encourage them to practice up to ten times a day; perhaps just for 30–60 seconds at a time. They should practice at times when they are feeling OK, and not wait for an episode of anxiety. If they do that, it will not be helpful. However, if they practice regularly, they will develop a body memory of how it feels and they can turn to it in a pinch.

The second technique to calm the body is *progressive muscle relaxation*. Again, this tool has been around for a long time. Some of my clients bring a voice recording device to a session. I lead them in a 10–15 minute relaxation session, which we record. They then can use the recording to create a sense of relaxation at any time they choose. A script of a typical relaxation exercise is provided in Handout 5-C.

The third technique is *visualization*. Human beings have a remarkable ability to create pictures in our minds. This is both a curse and a blessing. Traumatic memories can return to our consciousness without warning. On the other hand, we can also create mental pictures that trigger positive feelings. We can remember our last trip to the seashore and we can visualize some goal that we are striving to achieve. The amazing thing is that when we visualize something, our body reacts as if the event is really happening. That is why scary movies have the ability to make our hearts race and stomachs turn.

We can use that ability to our benefit by developing a list of pleasant scenes and calming images that we can focus on when we want to create a sense of peace and relaxation. Some visualization tips can be found in Handout 5-C.

HANDOUT 5-C
A TRIO OF TECHNIQUES TO CALM THE BODY

Deep Abdominal Breathing:

Deep abdominal breathing has long been known as an effective tool to reduce the physiological sensations of anxiety. That is why it is used in pain clinics, childbirth classes, yoga, and many meditative practices. The key is to learn how to breathe deeply from the abdomen. Once you have mastered the technique, you need to practice it for up to ten times a day. But you should practice when you are feeling OK. So, if you're waiting for the traffic light to change or your computer to boot up, take 30 seconds to take some deep breaths. If you do this, the technique will be more useful to you if you are confronted with an anxiety-provoking situation. Two simple breathing techniques are listed below. Once you have used these techniques to master the mechanics of deep breathing, you can practice breathing while standing, sitting or laying down.

Technique #1:

Stand up. Place both hands on lower stomach. As you inhale, imagine that your stomach is being blown up like a balloon. This allows the diaphragm to drop and enables air to flow all the way to the bottom of the lungs. As you inhale, your hands should move outward. Breathe in slowly to a count of four. Then, as you exhale, you draw your stomach in and your hands should move inward. Exhale slowly to a count of 4–6.

Technique #2:

Lie on your back on a flat surface. Place your right hand on your stomach and your left hand on your chest. As you inhale, your right hand should rise while your left hand remains relatively motionless. As you exhale, your right hand should fall. Breathe in slowly to a count of 4 and exhale to a count of 4–6.

Relaxation:

Following is a brief relaxation script. You are encouraged to record it (either in your own voice or using the voice of someone with whom you feel comfortable). You can listen to this recording as often as you like. Some people like to start their day with progressive relaxation; others like to practice it in the evening before they go to sleep. Try to disregard judgmental or negative thoughts such as "This isn't working," "I'm not getting relaxed enough," or "I'm not doing this right." Relaxation is a skill that you will develop gradually the more your practice it. In the meantime, be patient with yourself.

"Make sure you are wearing loose comfortable clothing. Find a comfortable position. You can do this exercise either sitting up or stretched out on your back—whichever is more comfortable. In order to eliminate visual distractions, close your eyes. Take a few deep abdominal breaths." (Pause a few seconds.)

"During this exercise, try not to judge or evaluate your experience. Don't trouble yourself with thoughts such as 'I wonder if I'm doing this right,' or 'I'm not getting relaxed enough.' Relaxation is a skill, and the more you practice, the better you will become."

"With your right hand, make a fist and flex your bicep muscle. Hold that tension. (Wait about 8–10 seconds.) When those muscles are ready to relax, let them relax. Let your hand and arm return to a comfortable position. Notice the contrast between the tension and the relaxation. Be aware of something very important. You created the tension, and you created the relaxation. Continue to take deep abdominal breaths, and let yourself relax." (Wait about 15 seconds.)

"Now do the same thing with your left hand and arm. Make a fist and flex your bicep muscle. Hold that tension. (Wait about 8–10 seconds.) When the muscle is ready to relax, let it relax. Let your hand and arm return to a comfortable position. Again, notice the contrast between the tension and the relaxation. Continue to take deep, slow abdominal breaths, and just let yourself relax." (Wait about 15 seconds.)

"Now tighten up all the muscles of your face. Hold that tension. (Wait 8–10 seconds.) When those muscles are ready to relax, let them relax. Again, notice the contrast between the tension and the relaxation. Continue to take deep, slow abdominal breaths and just relax." (Wait about 15 seconds.)

"Now work on the tension in your neck, chest, and upper back by shrugging your shoulders up. Hold that tension. (Wait 8–10 seconds.) When those muscles are ready to relax, let them relax. Again, notice the contrast between the tension and the relaxation." (Wait 15 seconds.)

"Now work on relaxing your back and stomach by arching your back up off of the bed (chair, floor, etc.). Hold that tension. (Wait 8–10 seconds.) When those muscles are ready to relax, let them relax and let your back return to a comfortable position." (Wait 15 seconds.)

"Now let's relax your right leg by stretching it out and pointing your toes away from your head. Hold that tension. (Wait 8–10 seconds.) When those muscles are ready to relax, let them relax. Now stretch your right leg out again, but this time turn your toes back toward your head and press your heel away from the head. This will gently stretch the hamstring muscle. (Wait 10 seconds.) When those muscles are ready to relax, let them relax." (Wait 15 seconds.)

"Now let's repeat this same procedure with the left leg. Stretch it out and point your toes away from your head. Hold that tension. (Wait 8–10 seconds.) When those muscles are ready to relax, let them relax. Now, stretch your left leg out but this time stretch out your heel so your toes point back toward your head. Hold that tension. (Wait 8–10 seconds.) When those muscles are ready to relax, let them relax. Again, notice the contrast between the tension and the relaxation. Continue to take deep, slow breaths. If you notice any tension in your body, just take note of it and let it melt away."

Visualization:

The human mind has a remarkable ability to see in pictures. The amazing thing is that when we have a picture in our mind, our bodies often respond as if the thing we are visualizing is actually happening. If you picture a time from your past that triggered strong emotions, you will likely re-experience the emotions as if the event was happening in the moment. This is why scary movies frighten us. This is why hearing a song that was popular when you were young will no doubt trigger memories and feelings from that time in your life. Take a moment now and try imagining sucking a lemon. You might even notice that your lips are puckered up as if you actually tasted the sour juice.

You are encouraged to record the following visualization exercise and incorporate it with the relaxation exercise previously recorded. If you combine all three tools for relaxation—breathing, relaxation, and visualization—you will find that they work very well together.

"Now that your body is relaxed, we are going to calm the mind. I invite you to go on an imaginary trip. I invite you to go someplace where you always feel relaxed and peaceful. This can be anyplace you choose. It can be someplace that you have actually visited. Or, it can be a place that you create in your mind. It can be a combination of places. It is completely your choice." (Pause a few seconds.)

"Go to that special place and enjoy it as thoroughly as you can. What do you see there? Are you there by yourself, or are there people you care about nearby? Perhaps they are people that you dearly love or revere. Either way is OK. What colors do you see? What objects to you see? Everything you see and everything you experience will simply serve to help you become more and more relaxed." (Pause a few seconds.)

"Make use of all of your senses. Are there any sounds in this place? Do you have any tactile sensations? Are there even any pleasant aromas associated with this place?" (Pause about 30 seconds.)

"Once you have thoroughly explored this special, relaxing place, you can prepare yourself to leave it to return to this time and place. You won't be too reluctant to leave it because you know that this wonderful, relaxing place is inside you and you can return to it anytime you want. Every time you return to this place, you will become even more relaxed, calm, and peaceful."

ACCEPTING AND EMBRACING PHYSIOLOGICAL SYMPTOMS

No doubt it is very beneficial to give clients the tools to calm and relax their bodies. However, I want to add a very important caveat. Yes, we try to relax the body, but we don't try too hard. We don't see it as something that **must** occur. If we focus on trying to relax at all costs, we experience a sense of failure if we don't achieve it. We put pressure on ourselves. "I have got to relax! I have got to relax!! **I have got to relax!!!**" For someone who is struggling and straining to control their physical sensations, this will likely only make the sensations stronger. After all, most of these reactions are involuntary, so we don't have much control over them.

What is more important is **to be OK even if the body isn't relaxed.** Now that we understand that these sensations are normal and harmless, we don't have to fear them. Sometimes it is better to accept and embrace them. Let them be!

People who struggle with anxiety have lost the ability to trust their bodies. We need to encourage them to trust their bodies and let them do what they are going to do.

When we exercise, we create many of the same physiological responses. When we ride a rollercoaster and watch a scary move, we experience many of the same sensations. Eventually, whatever physiological arousal we experience will pass. We don't have to fight it.

CREATING PHYSICAL SENSATIONS ON PURPOSE: INTEROCEPTIVE EXPOSURE

One way to learn not to struggle against physical sensations is to create them on purpose. This might seem strange, but that is exactly what many experts on anxiety disorders recommend. What better way to get comfortable with physical sensations than to make them happen? The term used to describe this technique is *interoceptive exposure*. The idea is to create these "symptoms" at a time when the client feels safe; this may be in the therapy office or at home with a loved one.

As you can imagine, this technique is often a tough sell. Clients hate these feelings! Why would they ever want to create them on purpose? I find it best to take a soft approach on this. If they absolutely do not want to do it, it's not required. However, I do encourage it as a way for them to make peace with their own bodies.

Of course, you want to make sure that clients do not have a medical condition that would make these techniques unsafe. Handout 5-D describes some simple techniques that they can try.

HANDOUT 5-D
CREATING PHYSICAL SENSATIONS ON PURPOSE: INTEROCEPTIVE EXPOSURE

Learning to Accept and Embrace Uncomfortable Physical Sensations
(Adapted from *The Mindfulness and Acceptance Workbook for Anxiety*)

I. Being willingly dizzy:

Stand 1–2 feet from a wall and stare at a spot for 2 minutes.

Use a swivel chair and spin yourself around as fast as possible.

While seated, place you head between your legs and then sit up quickly.

While standing, shake your head back and forth and side to side.

II. Being willingly out of breath:

Hold your breath for as long as you can.

Breathe through a straw.

Over-breathe: Rapidly inhale and exhale 30 times in 60 seconds.

III. Being willingly aerobic:

Walk fast.

Jog in place.

Climb steps.

Engage in any aerobic activity.

Note: If you have any medical condition that might be affected by these exercises, consult with your physician before attempting them.

THE ACT APPROACH: MINDFUL ACCEPTANCE

Earlier I briefly described the ACT approach to treating anxiety. The practitioners of ACT would say a loud "amen" to the idea of learning to embrace our physical sensations and not struggling to make them go away. We now understand that these sensations are not dangerous and we have almost no control over them anyway, so why not let them be? No matter how strong they are, they will soon pass.

The concepts of ACT may seem a bit strange and counterintuitive to clients at first. If something is troubling, our first impulse is to fight it, overcome it, and defeat it. There are many situations in which that approach works. For example, if I want to lose weight and be fit, it will take effort. I will have to work through discouragement. Passively accepting my current weight and fitness level would not be a good option.

However, in the arena of our inner thoughts and feelings, such striving and effort often works against us. For example, if we try very hard to not think of a pink elephant, we won't be able to do it.

Handout 5-E provides a brief description of the principles of ACT. Ask your clients to read it between sessions and discuss it with you during the next session. Handout 5-F describes some simple mindfulness meditations that clients can try on their own.

HANDOUT 5-E
BASIC PRINCIPLES OF ACCEPTANCE AND COMMITMENT THERAPY (ACT)

Mindfulness: This is the ability to be an observer of your inner life (thoughts, feelings, physical sensations) without being overly entangled with them or distressed by them. Thoughts, feelings, and physical sensations are things we experience, but they do not define who we are. We are not the victims of our inner experiences. We recognize that thoughts and feelings come and go. Whatever we might be feeling one moment, we are likely to be feeling something different a short time later.

For example, suppose I make an unfortunate social blunder. My automatic thoughts would probably include, "They think I'm an idiot," and I would feel quite embarrassed. At that point, I have a choice. I can internalize these thoughts and feelings, dwell on them, and continue to suffer. Or, I can be aware of them and let them pass. Perhaps I could ask myself what I could learn from the experience, and then let go of my self-critical and judgmental thoughts.

Acceptance: Not only do we want to be mindful or our experience, we want to approach it with an attitude of kindness, compassion, and self-acceptance. We want to embrace experience rather than struggle against it. This concept is particularly helpful in dealing with anxiety. What do you do when you first notice feelings of anxiety? Do you criticize yourself for your feelings and struggle to suppress them? If so, you might have noticed that this only makes your anxiety worse. However, if you can accept and embrace your anxious feelings, they are less of a problem for you.

Commitment: Thoughts and feelings come and go. We do not have much control over our automatic thoughts or the initial feelings that they trigger. However, we always have control over our behavior. No matter how anxious, angry, or sad I am, I can always choose how I will respond to these feelings. Will the feelings themselves dictate what I do, or will I choose to behave in ways that are consistent with my values?

A basic premise of ACT is that, as much as possible, we want to make behavioral choices based on our values. We want to be guided by the commitments that we have made to ourselves and others.

For example, let's say that you feel anxious at social gatherings. In spite of this, you have been invited to a birthday party for a very close friend. Your anxiety will tell you not to go. However, you deeply value this relationship and know that it will mean a lot to your friend if you attend. So, how do you decide? Do you let fear dictate what you do, or do you act in accordance to how you value this relationship?

HANDOUT 5-F
SIMPLE MINDFULNESS MEDITATIONS

The key element in mindfulness is the willingness to be an observer of our inner thoughts, feelings, and physical sensations without taking any of them too seriously. Our minds are continuously presenting us with thoughts and feelings, many of which are random and not of much use to us. We need to consider it data that we can use or discard as it suits us. Another way to see it is to imagine that your thoughts and feelings are going past you like a train. You can observe the train but you don't have to jump on board.

Here are a few simple mindfulness exercises that were adapted from a number of sources. As you did with the relaxation techniques, you might want to record these meditations and listen to one or two of them on a daily basis.

Mindful Breathing: "Start by getting into a comfortable position and allow your eyes to close. For the next few moments, focus your attention on your breathing. Notice how it feels as you breathe in and breathe out. Notice how your chest and stomach rise and fall as you breathe. There is no need to change your breathing in any way. Just notice it. The goal is to just be aware. At some point you may notice that your mind has drifted away from your breathing to other thoughts and feelings. This is not a mistake; this is just what minds do. When you become aware that your mind has drifted to something else, just take note of it, and gently guide your awareness back to your breathing. Try to adopt an attitude of kindness and acceptance toward your experience. If you notice critical or judgmental thoughts, take note of them as well, and then gently escort your awareness back to your breathing. Try to gently accept whatever thoughts and feelings arise. There is no goal, no right or wrong way to do this. The goal is to just be aware. When you are ready, open your eyes. Make a decision to bring this same attitude of kind acceptance to the rest of your day."

Mindfulness of Sounds: "Sit in a comfortable position and close your eyes. For the next few moments, allow your awareness to focus on any sounds around you. Do not try to make yourself hear anything; just take note of any sounds that you experience. You may notice sounds that you hadn't noticed before. Take note of the different kinds of sounds. Some may be close; some may be far away. From time to time, you may notice that your awareness has shifted to other thoughts and feelings. If you notice this, congratulate yourself for being mindful and gently escort your mind back to the sounds around you. As best you can, accept your thoughts and feelings without judgment. But if you find yourself being judgmental, congratulate yourself for being mindful and gently guide your awareness back to the sounds around you. Do this for as long as you feel comfortable, and when you are ready, open your eyes and make a decision to bring kindness and compassion to whatever you experience for the rest of your day."

Mindful Walking: "Take a few moments to go for a walk. As you do, allow yourself to take note of anything you experience. Notice how your body feels as you walk. Notice the rhythm of your walking. Take note of what your see as you walk. Take it all in as if you have never seen these things before. Take note of what you hear. Take these sounds in as if you have never heard them before. Also be aware of any thoughts and feelings that arise as you walk. Accept whatever comes to your mind. As best you can, just notice these thoughts and feelings without judgment. But if you notice judgmental thoughts, just take note of them and gently guide your awareness back to your walking. There is no goal; no right or wrong way to do this. Be kind to yourself and accept whatever you experience. Continue walking for as long as you wish. As you finish your walk, encourage yourself to maintain this attitude of kindness and self-acceptance for the rest of your day."

Clouds: "Imagine that you are outside on a lovely day. The sky is mostly clear but there are a number of clouds that are gently and slowly passing overhead. As best you can, focus your attention on the clouds as they pass by. Do not try to make the clouds move slower or faster, just let them pass over as they may. As you observe the clouds, take note of any thoughts, feelings, or physical sensations that you experience. As best you can, avoid judging yourself for whatever you experience. Instead, imagine these thoughts, feelings, and physical sensations are in the clouds that are slowly passing overhead. Observe each thought, feeling, and physical sensation as it slowly drifts out of sight. When new thoughts, feelings, and physical sensations arise, place each of them on a cloud and watch as they drift away as well. As you finish this exercise, make a decision to adopt an attitude of kind acceptance to whatever you experience during the rest of your day."

So now we have discussed the physiological aspect of anxiety. We have learned that the physical sensations of anxiety are a normal response to a perceived threat that isn't there. These sensations are not harmful or dangerous in any way. We can encourage our clients to accept and embrace these responses, while also giving them practical tools to help reduce them if they so desire. Now we move on to explore the relationship between our thoughts and our feelings.

Chapter Six: The Cognitive Component

Cognitive Therapy was the brainchild of Dr. Aaron Beck. Dr. David Burns popularized the principles of Cognitive Therapy in his best-selling books, *Feeling Good* and *The Feeling Good Handbook*. More recently, the principles of Cognitive Therapy have been combined with some of our traditional Behavioral Therapies and subsumed under the title Cognitive Behavioral Therapy (CBT). CBT has a well-established track record and is generally recognized as the treatment of choice for most anxiety problems.

CBT practitioners have observed that we all have certain habits of thinking that add to our stress. Life is hard enough, but often the way we think about things makes it worse. In the writings of Beck, Burns, and others, these unfortunate thinking habits are called "Cognitive Distortions." I have never much cared for that term because it sounds a bit insulting, as if the person's thinking is crazy or abnormal.

More recently, the term "Automatic Negative Thoughts," or ANTS, has been put forth as a way of describing these mental habits. I much prefer the term ANTS because it more accurately describes what is going on.

Many of our thoughts are "automatic" in that we don't intend to think them. They just pop into our minds if something triggers them. For example, if I say, "Twinkle, twinkle, little …," your mind can't help but think "star." You are probably not thinking about the name of your high school, but …" Again, I'm sure that the name of your school came into your awareness. We don't seek out our Automatic Thoughts; we don't intend to think them; they just come to us.

It only stands to reason that some of our thoughts will be negative, so having ANTS does not make us irrational or crazy. As I tell my clients, "I've got ANTS. You've got ANTS. All God's children got ANTS."

Having ANTS is not the problem. It's how we interpret them. Do we see them as "just those pesky ANTS," or do we believe them, own them, and see them as representing absolute truth? For example, I mentioned earlier that while writing this book, the thought "I'm never going to finish this" came into my mind. If I believed that the thought represented "reality," I would feel discouraged, depressed, and possibly give up. However, if I replace that thought with, "I'm making progress; I have a good chance of making it," I will be hopeful and not discouraged. It's all in how I think.

It is very important to familiarize clients with these basic ideas. They need to learn that by changing their thinking, they can often change their feelings, and live more fulfilling lives. I have a number of handouts that I use to educate clients on CBT. The first is Handout 6-A.

At all times, it is essential to normalize the fact that everyone has ANTS. We can't help it! Often clients will put themselves down for their ANTS. "I'm fortune telling again. I'm so stupid." Basically, they are having ANTS about their ANTS. Start reciting the famous nursery rhyme "Mary had a little …." It's impossible not to think "lamb." The problem is not that we have ANTS; it's our tendency to believe them and take them too seriously that is the problem.

HANDOUT 6-A
PRINCIPLES OF COGNITIVE BEHAVIORAL THERAPY (CBT):
CHANGING OUR FEELINGS BY CHANGING OUR THINKING

This is the most important principle; every succeeding principle depends on it. Here's an illustration: You are driving to a job interview and are stuck in traffic. What you feel in that situation will depend on what you think. If you think, "This is terrible. Nothing ever works out for me. I'll never get a job," you will be pretty upset.

But let's say your thoughts are something like "I need to learn from this and leave earlier next time. All I can do is get there as soon as I can and try to explain to them what happened. I hope they'll understand." You're still not going to be happy, but you'll be a little less upset.

That is not to say that choosing your response is easy. We all have habits of thinking that are so engrained that they are "automatic." We don't intend to think this way. We might not even be aware of the thoughts. Nevertheless, they are always there. Many of these thinking habits are negative, so we refer to them as ANTS (Automatic Negative Thoughts). Much of our unhappiness is caused by our ANTS. It's not that ANTS are completely wrong; they often have an element of truth. But they also contain lies; lies that we tell ourselves.

So you've got ANTS; I've got ANTS; all God's children got ANTS. There is no point in being ashamed of them or even trying to stop them. The mind doesn't know how to NOT think something (e.g., try real hard to NOT think of a pink elephant), so any effort you make to get your ANTS to go away is bound to backfire.

What you can control is how you choose to respond to your ANTS. Do you take them as absolute truth or can you allow yourself to explore a different way of thinking? It is your CHOICE where you go from there.

That is why I say "in the end" you choose your response. You might not be able to control the first flash of emotion, but all human beings have the capacity to stop, reflect, and figure out how they want to think and feel about any situation.

So when you are upset, wait! Become aware of your ANTS and use your human capacity to think things through. Your distress will be lessened and you will be more likely to find an effective solution to the problem. However, if you continue to feed your ANTS with more negative thinking, your distress will increase and no solution will be found.

VARIETIES OF ANTS

It is helpful for clients to understand the different varieties of ANTS that have been identified by CBT practitioners. I give my clients a handout that describes and provides examples of all the different varieties (Handout 6-B). Let's review some of our most popular ANTS.

Fortune Telling: When we are anxious, we are probably predicting some bad event or outcome. We might not be completely aware of what it is, but it invariably is there. Examples might be, "My mind will go blank during my presentation," "I won't pass the test," or (my favorite) "I'm never going to finish this book." Sometimes the feared event is something specific (failing the test) and sometimes it is more vague ("Something bad is going to happen."). Sometimes what we are predicting is anxiety itself ("I just know I'll be too anxious to do that.").

Catastrophic Thinking: This is fortune telling on steroids. Not only will the outcome be bad; it will be awful and unbearable. If my thought is "If I don't get this job, I'm going to end up homeless," or "I will die if I have another panic attack," I might be engaging in catastrophic thinking.

Mind Reading: We assume that people are having negative thoughts about us. At a party my thoughts are, "These people don't like me." If you have to give a brief talk to some co-workers, you think, "They will be able to tell that I'm anxious and I will make a fool of myself." When we think this way, we turn every social event into a performance during which we must control the thoughts of other people. Mind reading is the cause of social anxiety.

All or None Thinking: We think in rigid, black or white categories. If we don't score 100 on the test, we feel like a complete failure. If someone doesn't like something about me, they dislike everything about me. This can lead to anxious perfectionism and low self-esteem.

Overgeneralization: One or two events make us believe that something is "always" or "never" true. Here are some common examples: "Nothing ever works out for me." "I'm always messing up." "I'm never going to succeed at this." Overgeneralization is often the basis for pessimism, negativity, discouragement, and low self-esteem.

Mental Filter: We focus on the most negative aspect of a situation and fail to notice what might be more positive (or at least neutral). For example, you get a number of positive responses to your presentation, but all you can think about is the one critical response. You focus on one undesirable trait and lose sight of your positive qualities. If you have free time, all you can think about is how bored you are and don't look for positive things to do. If you are stuck in heavy traffic, you focus on how "awful" it is that you have to wait and don't think about how nice it is to have a car. This is the "glass half-empty" approach. Mental filter is often the basis for depression, pessimism, discouragement, and low self-esteem.

"Should" Thoughts: When we think this way, we are requiring the world, other people, and even ourselves to live up to our expectations. It is an unwillingness to accept what is. I am angry at you because you "should" have remembered my birthday. I feel guilty and inadequate because I "should" be making more money. "Should" thoughts about others provoke anger; "should" thoughts toward ourselves provoke guilt.

Labeling: We apply negative labels toward others and ourselves. The list of labels is endless: lazy, stupid, rude, insensitive, overly sensitive, and so on. In reality, labels are not accurate because no one is always lazy, stupid, rude, etc. When we label ourselves, we feel guilty or inadequate. When we label others, we feel angry.

Discounting the Positive: We minimize the significance of our accomplishments, successes, and blessings. Somehow, they just "don't count." "Yes, I won the tennis match, but my opponent had a bad day." "Yes, I was accepted by many colleges, but I didn't get into the best ones." "Yes, I got the promotion, but there wasn't much competition."

Emotional Reasoning: We believe that our emotions are an accurate reflection of reality. In the middle of a panic attack, I feel like "I'm going crazy" or "I have to get out of here." Because I feel like a "loser," I must be one. If I feel rejected, I must have been rejected. Since I feel guilty, I must have done something wrong.

HANDOUT 6-B
VARIETIES OF AUTOMATIC NEGATIVE THOUGHTS (ANTS)

A. Fortune Telling: We are predicting that something bad will happen. We will flunk out of school, lose our job, or catch a serious disease. Often we are overestimating the likelihood that the bad thing will happen. Fortune telling is the basis of almost all anxiety and worry.

B. Catastrophic Thinking: This often goes along with fortune telling. Not only will the bad thing happen, but the consequences will be terrible. We are overestimating the consequence of the bad event and underestimating our ability to cope. So, it would be "terrible" if we are late or "awful" if we get a low grade on a test. Minor failings, setbacks, frustrations, and mistakes are seen as more awful than they really are. Catastrophic thinking is the basis for severe anxiety.

C. Mind Reading: We assume that people are having negative thoughts about us. At a party my thoughts are, "These people don't like me." If you have to give a brief talk to some co-workers, you think, "They will be able to tell that I'm anxious and I will make a fool of myself." When we think this way, we turn every social event into a performance during which we must control the thoughts of other people. Mind reading is the cause of social anxiety.

D. All or None Thinking: We think in rigid, black or white categories. If we don't score 100 on the test, we feel like a complete failure. If someone doesn't like something about me, they dislike everything about me. This can lead to anxious perfectionism and low self-esteem.

E. Overgeneralization: One or two events make us believe that something is "always" or "never" true. Here are some common examples: "Nothing ever works out for me." "I'm always messing up." "I'm never going to succeed at this." Overgeneralization is often the basis for pessimism, negativity, discouragement, and low self-esteem.

F. Mental Filter: We focus on the most negative aspect of a situation and fail to notice what might be more positive (or at least neutral). For example, you get a number of positive responses to your presentation, but all you can think about is the one critical response. You focus on one undesirable trait and lose sight of your positive qualities. If you have free time, all you can think about is how bored you are and don't look for positive things to do. If you are stuck in heavy traffic, you focus on how "awful" it is that you have to wait and don't think about how nice it is to have a car. This is the "glass half-empty" approach. Mental filter is often the basis for depression, pessimism, discouragement, and low self-esteem.

G. "Should" Thoughts: When we think this way, we are requiring the world, other people, and even ourselves to live up to our expectations. It is an unwillingness to accept what is. I am angry at you because you "should" have remembered my birthday. I feel guilty and inadequate because I "should" be making more money. "Should" thoughts about others provoke anger; "should" thoughts toward ourselves provoke guilt.

H. Labeling: We apply negative labels toward others and ourselves. The list of labels is endless: lazy, stupid, rude, insensitive, overly sensitive, and so on. In reality, labels are not accurate because no one is always lazy, stupid, rude, etc. When we label ourselves, we feel guilty or inadequate. When we label others, we feel angry.

I. Discounting the Positive: We minimize the significance of our accomplishments, successes, and blessings. Somehow, they just "don't count." "Yes, I won the tennis match, but my opponent had a bad day." "Yes, I was accepted by many colleges, but I didn't get into the best ones." "Yes, I got the promotion, but there wasn't much competition."

J. Emotional Reasoning: We believe that our emotions are an accurate reflection of reality. In the middle of a panic attack, I feel like "I'm going crazy" or "I have to get out of here." Because I feel like a "loser," I must be one. If I feel rejected, I must have been rejected. Since I feel guilty, I must have done something wrong.

THE FOUR CORE MENTAL BIASES OF ANXIETY

If you gather all the various ANTS that contribute to anxiety and look for common themes, you will almost always discover that the individual is engaging in one or more of the following mental biases.

1. We might be overestimating the likelihood that the bad thing will happen. Often what we fear is a very uncommon event, but our thinking gives us the idea that it is definitely going to happen. Someone who is afraid of elevators may fear that the elevator will get stuck and they will be "trapped," and thus will suffer an unbearable panic attack—even though elevators rarely get stuck.

2. We might be overestimating the consequences should the bad thing happen. Yes, bad things happen, but we might think that the consequences would be more dire than they really would be. How often have we felt that something would be "awful" when it really wasn't so bad? For example, when I am going somewhere I like to be sure that I arrive on time, if not early. Sometimes, it's very important that I do so, such as when I have an important business appointment or I'm catching a plane. However, there has been many a time when I have stressed myself over arriving on time when it really wasn't all that important.

3. We might be underestimating our ability to cope should the bad thing happen. Often when we are highly anxious, we forget that we have experiences and skills to help us cope with the bad outcome. We feel helpless. We tell ourselves that we "couldn't stand it," or "would just fall apart" if things don't turn out that way we want. For example, clients with severe panic disorder often believe that they just can't tolerate it if they have another attack. Even though they know that the symptoms are harmless, and even though they have breathing and other tools to cope, they see themselves as completely incapable of getting through the attack unscathed. Another example is a person who is concerned about losing his job and is convinced that he won't be able to find another one if he is laid off.

4. We might be having great difficulty accepting uncertainty. There are things that could **possibly** happen (e.g., the elevator gets stuck), but **probably won't**. Sometimes when we are highly anxious, we are insisting on complete certainty. It's not enough for it to be unlikely to happen; we have to know for certain. People with severe worry problems will focus on every possible negative outcome, and unless they can know for certain that it will not occur, they will worry about it. However, certainty is rarely found in this world and all of us have to learn to live with uncertainty.

I like to share these common biases with my clients to see if they might be engaging in any of them. Again, I make the point that these are common things that everyone does to some extent. You can use Handout 6-C as an aid to this discussion.

HANDOUT 6-C
THE FOUR CORE MENTAL BIASES OF ANXIETY

If you gather all the various ANTS that contribute to anxiety and look for common themes, you will almost always discover that the individual is engaging in one or more of the following mental biases. Look over this list, and see if you recognize any of these habits of thinking. Remember, everyone engages in this type of thinking sometimes, so there is no need to criticize yourself for having these thoughts.

1. We might be overestimating the likelihood that the bad thing will happen. Often what we fear is a very uncommon event, but our thinking gives us the idea that it is definitely going to happen. Someone who is afraid of elevators may fear that the elevator will get stuck and they will be "trapped," and thus will suffer an unbearable panic attack—even though elevators rarely get stuck.

2. We might be overestimating the consequences should the bad thing happen. Yes, bad things happen, but we might think that the consequences would be more dire than they really would be. How often have we felt that something would be "awful" when it really wasn't so bad? For example, when I am going somewhere I like to be sure that I arrive on time, if not early. Sometimes, it's very important that I do so, such as when I have an important business appointment or I'm catching a plane. However, there has been many a time when I have stressed myself over arriving on time when it really wasn't all that important.

3. We might be underestimating our ability to cope should the bad thing happen. Often when we are highly anxious, we forget that we have experiences and skills to help us cope with the bad outcome. We feel helpless. We tell ourselves that we "couldn't stand it," or "would just fall apart" if things don't turn out that way we want. For example, people with severe panic disorder often believe that they just can't tolerate it if they have another attack. Even though they know that the symptoms are harmless, and even though they have breathing and other tools to cope, they see themselves as completely incapable of getting through the attack unscathed. Another example is a person who is concerned about losing his job and is convinced that he won't be able to find another one if he is laid off.

4. We might be having great difficulty accepting uncertainty. There are things that could possibly happen (e.g., the elevator gets stuck), but probably won't. Sometimes when we are highly anxious, we are insisting on complete certainty. It's not enough for it to be unlikely to happen; we have to know for certain. People with severe worry problems will focus on every possible negative outcome and unless they can know for certain that it will not occur, they will worry about it. However, certainty is rarely found in this world and all of us have to learn to live with uncertainty.

THE ART AND SCIENCE OF CBT: IDENTIFY AND COUNTER ANTS

At the beginning, CBT looks much any other style of psychotherapy. The research conducted by Carl Rogers and others in the 1950s is still valid. The basic therapist qualities of empathy, concreteness, and unconditional positive regard are still essential. If clients don't feel heard, understood, and respected, they won't stick around.

After clients have had the opportunity to express their concerns and you have gathered any relevant history, it is useful to introduce the basic principles of CBT. I tell them that I make use of a number of different approaches in helping clients. I then go on to say that I have been particularly impressed by the usefulness of CBT and plan to use it quite a bit during our sessions.

I then entertain any questions or concerns that they might have about my approach. Today, many clients have heard of CBT and know that it is effective in treating anxiety and other conditions. However, some might be skeptical. They have seen portrayals of therapy in movies and TV in which the therapist delves into the client's unconscious. Then, there is a dramatic moment of insight in which the client uncovers some deeply hidden memory. This leads to an intense emotional release and the client is essentially cured on the spot.

I tell these clients that we will be talking about their life history, and they may develop a new understanding of how their current concerns have been shaped by their past experiences. Everyone has a story to tell and it is important to explore the narrative of a person's life. However, I suggest that our primary concern will be what is causing them distress now and preventing them from enjoying life to the fullest.

At the end of the first or second session, I give them a copy of my handouts that describe the basic concepts and the varieties of ANTS. I also have a handout with a case study that illustrates what we will be doing (see Handout 6-D). I ask them to look it over and tell them we will discuss it during our next session.

Daniel was a 32-year-old office worker who struggled with anxiety and low self-esteem. During one session, he described some problems he had with his mother-in-law. Their relationship had always been somewhat distant and awkward and he never felt quite accepted by her. I asked him to write down some of his thoughts about his mother-in-law. He had several but the first two were: "She hates me." "She wants me to know that she hates me."

He gave me permission to ask questions about his thoughts. First, I asked him if he noticed any varieties of ANTS. He was able to identify "mind reading" because he was assuming that he knew his mother-in-law's thoughts. It was also an example of "all-or-none thinking" because he was assuming that she completely hated him and had no positive thoughts about him at all.

I then asked, "Except for how you feel, what is the evidence that she hates you?" He described a couple incidents that might have been interpreted as slights, but it wasn't at all clear if that is what she intended. I then asked, "What is the evidence that she doesn't hate you?" He described several pleasant conversations that they had had, and how he had helped her with a problem she was having.

I then asked, "Do you think she completely hates you, that you have no worth at all?" He had to admit that he really didn't know for sure how she felt about him, but he doubted that she hated him completely. She probably had mixed feelings about him.

As we discussed this further, he decided that it was OK if she had mixed feelings about him. After all, he had mixed feelings about her, so how could he expect her to feel otherwise?

I went on to ask, "So, if it is your best guess that she had mixed feelings about you, what choices do you have about how you respond to that?" We decided that he had two choices: (1) He could sulk, feel sorry for himself, and nurse a grudge against her. (2) He could accept it and work to build the best relationship with her that he could. He chose the second option.

You will notice that I didn't argue with him because I didn't know how she felt about him. My goal was to help him see that he had a choice about how to navigate this relationship.

When clients return for the next session, and if they have read the material (If they haven't, you have a motivational issue, so remember your Motivational Interviewing), they typically will tell you that they have many ANTS. Often, they will tell you this with great embarrassment because it confirms to them how really messed up they are. It is crucial at this point to normalize ANTS as something EVERYONE experiences. I often share some of my own favorites. I tell them that by being self-critical, they are essentially having ANTS about their ANTS. The problem is not the ANTS themselves, but how we interpret and respond to them.

After clients have been educated on the basic ideas of CBT, the next step is to ask them to describe a current or recent event/situation/issue that triggered a high level of distress. It is crucial that you show empathy and affirm the validity of the client's feelings. Often inexperienced CBT clinicians jump right in and start questioning the client's thoughts and feelings. I can't overstate what a mistake that is. Good CBT is not arguing against or debating the client's experience. In fact, it is a waste of time to try to talk someone out of their feelings. If a friend is worried, and you say, "You shouldn't worry," does that change their mind? Definitely not! If you are married, the next time your spouse is angry at you, say, "You shouldn't be angry." I cannot imagine any spouse saying, "Thank you so much for pointing out my irrational thinking."

Once clients have described the situation, ask them to describe as specifically as they can what their thoughts were in the situation. Sometime clients will have difficulty identifying thoughts. They might say, "I wasn't thinking anything; I was just very upset." When clients do that, acknowledge that they might not have been aware of any thoughts in the moment. But, looking back, can they imagine what they might have been thinking? Or, what might someone else in an identical situation be thinking? Or, another way to put it would be, "We are always silently talking to ourselves. What do you think you might have been saying to yourself?"

As clients identify their thoughts, I ask them to write them down. I have a pad and pen that I keep handy for that purpose. Writing down thoughts allows clients to develop some perspective on their thinking—mindfulness, if you will.

After clients have identified their thoughts, I **ask permission** to explore their thoughts with them and ask questions that might help them think/feel differently. Why do I ask permission? It is just another way in which I want to affirm and respect the client's autonomy.

The key art and technique of CBT is in the process of Socratic questioning. It is not a question of convincing them to think differently; it is asking powerful questions which will allow them to decide if they want to think differently.

Here are some powerful questions that can help clients challenge their ANTS. I call them the ANT-eaters:

> "What ANTS do you recognize in your thoughts?"
>
> "Apart from how you feel, what is the evidence that your thought is accurate? What is the evidence that it isn't accurate?"
>
> "Are you 100 percent convinced that your thought is accurate?"
>
> "What is the worst thing that could happen? If it happens, how will you cope with it? If it happens, what would still be good in your life?"
>
> "Are there other outcomes that are possible?"
>
> "What are other possible explanations for what happened?"

"What would you tell a valued friend who thought this way?"

"What might other people think about this?"

"What part of this do you have control over?"

"What are the advantages of thinking this way? What are the disadvantages?"

After going through this questioning process, ask clients to think of alternative thoughts that they might have about the situation. It is not necessary that their alternative thoughts be completely positive. It is enough if they are realistic, perhaps less negative, and help them realize that there is always another way to look at things.

It is also important to note that the goal is not for clients to always feel good. We are not creating emotionless robots. There will always be circumstances that will trigger intense feelings of sadness, anger, anxiety, and guilt. Life is tough and negative feelings come along with it. The goal is to help clients experience normal levels of emotion and be able to cope with them productively.

Once you have gone through this process a time or two, you can encourage clients to do their own ANT hunting. Ask them to notice situations that trigger distress, identify their ANTS, ask challenging questions, and develop alternative thoughts. I give them Handout 6-E to help them think about questions to ask themselves. I encourage them to make copies of Handout 6-F to help them apply CBT ideas to any distressing events that occur.

HANDOUT 6-E
QUESTIONS TO CHALLENGE OUR NEGATIVE THOUGHTS

Aside from how you feel, what is the evidence that your negative thought is true? What is the evidence that it is not true?

Are you 100 percent certain that your fear is true? If not, what is the real chance?

If your predicted bad outcome occurs, what will be the real consequences of it? How might you best cope with those consequences? What will still be good in your life?

What ANTS do you recognize in your thoughts?

Apart from how you feel, what is the evidence that your thought is accurate? What is the evidence that it isn't accurate?

Are there other outcomes that are possible?

What are other possible explanations for what happened?

What would you tell a valued friend who thought this way?

What might other people think about this?

What part of this do you have control over?

What are the advantages of thinking this way? What are the disadvantages?

How much will this matter a year from now?

What practical steps can you take to affect the outcome?

What are alternative explanations for what happened?

Given what has happened, what are your options for responding to it?

LET'S GO ANT HUNTING: APPLYING COGNITIVE BEHAVIORAL THERAPY

Describe the situation:

_____

_____

_____

What negative emotions did you feel? (e.g., anxiety, worry, anger, sadness, guilt, shame, etc.)

_____

_____

_____

What were your thoughts?

_____

_____

_____

What varieties of ANTS do you notice? (e.g., fortune telling, mind reading, etc.)

_____

_____

_____

What questions can you ask yourself about your ANTS? (e.g., "Except for how you feel, what is the evidence that your thought is accurate? What is the evidence that it is not accurate?" See Handout 6-E for a list of ANT-eater questions.)

_____

_____

_____

What might be some alternative ways for you to think about this? What thoughts could you use to replace your ANTS?

_____

_____

_____

DIGGING DEEPER: DISCOVERING HIDDEN ASSUMPTIONS

In helping clients identify and counter their ANTS, you will often notice them having the same troubling thoughts and feelings over and over again. They will employ CBT principles to make themselves feel better about one situation, only to find themselves struggling with the same issues shortly thereafter.

The reason for this is that we all have certain underlying belief systems or biases that determine how we think and feel in any situation. We might be vaguely aware of some of these underlying beliefs or we might be totally unaware of them. CBT practitioners have various terms to describe these cognitive biases. They sometimes are called "schemas," "core beliefs," "self-defeating attitudes," or "hidden assumptions." I sometimes refer to them as ANT colonies because they are "underground" and the ANTS emerge from them.

When you are able to help clients identify their hidden assumptions, you have struck therapeutic gold. At this point, CBT begins to look a lot like psychodynamic therapies, in that we are helping clients identify underlying attitudes of which they might not be aware.

As an example, let's return to the young man we previously discussed who was having negative feelings about his mother-in-law. Only the week before, he described a situation in which he had been similarly offended by a supervisor at work. On yet another occasion, he experienced similar thoughts and feelings about a family member. After the third situation, I asked him if he saw any connections between the three. His reply was to identify the hidden assumption, "People don't respect me." Having identified that as an issue, we had much to talk about in therapy. Where did he first get that idea? What would it take for him to change his belief?

As therapists, our job is to notice hidden assumptions and gently bring them to the client's attention. However, we must always remember that our observations are only tentative hypotheses and not absolute facts. We must never push our interpretation on clients, or label them as "resistant" if they disagree. We might be dead wrong. Even if our hypotheses are accurate, clients might not be in a position to recognize it at this point.

There are as many hidden assumptions as there are people, so it would be impossible to provide an exhaustive list. However, I have a list of some of my favorites that I provide for my clients. You can find my list in Handout 6-G.

Perhaps you find yourself having the same ANTS and experiencing the same troubling emotions over and over. You dispute your ANTS in one situation, only to find them plaguing you in another.

You may feel tempted to criticize yourself about your negative thinking (i.e., have ANTS about your ANTS), but there is no need to do so.

The same ANTS come back to you repeatedly because we all have certain underlying beliefs that influence how we think and feel about any situation. Cognitive behavioral therapists have several terms to describe these underlying belief patterns or biases. Some use the term "schemas," while others use the term "core beliefs." I like the term "hidden assumptions." Sometimes, I refer to these as the "ANT colonies" because they are "underground" and the ANTS emerge out of them.

We might be vaguely aware of these underlying beliefs, but often we do not recognize them until someone points them out to us. Even then, we may be reluctant to take an objective look at ourselves and see how our thinking may be adding to our distress.

Just like with ANTS, there is no need to beat yourself up for having these hidden assumptions. Everyone has them! The key is the willingness to identify what they are and then make a conscious decision as to whether or not you want to change them.

There are as many different hidden assumptions as there are people, but following are a few common ones.

"Things must turn out the way I want." It is natural to want things your way, but when you think that they must be your way, you are setting yourself up for frustration. There are things we can control and things we can't, so we can't always expect things to go our way. A secret of happiness is to be able to adapt to difficult situations. A healthier perspective would be, "I will do what I can to make things turn out my way, but I will adapt if they don't."

"People should meet my expectations." Much of our anger and hurt feelings come from expecting someone to behave the way we want. If you expect a friend to remember your birthday, you will be hurt if she doesn't. If you expect your spouse to always listen to you attentively, you will be angry when he doesn't. It is natural to have expectations, but we are wise to not hold on to them tightly. I find it best to focus on my behavior. Am I treating people honorably? Am I expressing my wishes clearly and respectfully? If so, then that is all I can do. I cannot control what someone else does.

"It's always my fault." It is always wise to take responsibility for our actions. It does no good to blame other people or outside influences (e.g., the economy) for our problems. However, neither is it helpful to heap criticism on ourselves when things turn out badly. A hallmark of maturity is the ability to recognize our part in the problem, learn from our mistakes, and do our best to accept the consequences. Having done that, do we really need to berate ourselves?

"It's never my fault, it's always your (their) fault." Some people cannot tolerate any criticism and will deflect it in any way possible. This sensitivity to criticism may stem from other self-defeating attitudes such as "It is awful to be criticized," or "Any criticism at all means that I am inadequate." When we hold these beliefs, we come off as arrogant and we don't give ourselves the opportunity to honestly look at ourselves and learn from our mistakes.

"People are against me." I hear this all the time. "My boss has it in for me." "No one in the church talks to me." "The teacher picks on me." In almost any social setting, they see themselves as being discriminated against. They feel that they are the victim or scapegoat. They can cite many incidences to support their belief, but they do not notice anything good that happens to them. Of course, there can sometimes be some truth to their perceptions, but it is often their own negative attitude that has led to their being disliked. A wise person once told me, "People don't do things against you; they do them for themselves." I find it useful to assume that people are at least neutral toward me until I have clear evidence to the contrary. If I have clear evidence that someone doesn't like me, I will consider my options. Should I try to change their perception or can I accept their negative opinion?

"Any failure is a sign of my inadequacy." Any worthwhile endeavor involves some element of risk. In spite of our best efforts, we might fail to reach our goal. Some people believe that any failure is so shameful that they don't want to try anything if there is any chance of failures. They use this fear of failure as an excuse not to try anything worthwhile. Many dreams are never fulfilled because the fear of failure got in the way.

"I'm not as good as other people." An unfortunate human habit is comparing ourselves to others and believing that we don't stack up. Other people are smarter, better looking, or have achieved a higher level of success. This self-defeating attitude is the source of much of our misery. If someone points out a strength we "discount the positive" by minimizing its importance. It really makes no sense to compare ourselves to others. If you envy your wealthy relative, will your life really be better if he loses his fortune? So why compare yourself to him? If you want to work to make more money, do so. But do it because it's important to you, not to keep up with your relative.

"I'm better than others." This is sometimes difficult to see because no one wants to admit to arrogance or self-righteousness. Instead, this attitude reveals itself in other ways. In pointing out how our co-workers don't get along, we are suggesting that we are somehow above such pettiness. In describing the challenges we are facing, we are subtly pointing out how noble and long-suffering we are. I am all for healthy self-esteem, but we create problems for ourselves when we see ourselves as fundamentally different from the rest of humanity.

"I can't stand this." "This is awful." "I wouldn't be able to stand it if …" All of these phrases suggest a perceived inability (or unwillingness) to endure anything that might be difficult, challenging, or troubling. A person says he will "go crazy" if he doesn't have anything to do. Someone else says it is "awful" to be rejected or to be alone. We all wish that life was always rosy, but it just isn't. Things happen that are inconvenient, unfortunate, disappointing, embarrassing, or frustrating. Yet very few things happen that we can't adapt to, bounce back from, or even grow from. Yes, we do our best to prevent bad things from happening, but it's rarely the end of the world if they do.

"I have to please everybody else. It is awful to be disliked or rejected." Have you ever noticed that even though you didn't like a particular person, you still wanted them to like you? Some of us will go to any length to avoid the disapproval of others. This includes a kind of "all or none thinking," which says "If they dislike anything about me, they dislike me completely." With this mindset, any social situation becomes a performance in which we try to control the thoughts of others. But how much control do we really have over the thoughts of others? This self-defeating attitude is at the core of most social anxiety. Sometimes, a person with this mindset will grow tired of this way of thinking and will switch to the opposite extreme: "Other people be damned! I don't care what they think!" This sounds very confident and brave, but people with this attitude come off as arrogant and abrasive and may suffer just as much as those who try too hard to please others. I think that balance is called for here. Yes, it's better to be liked and accepted, but it is not the end of the world if we aren't. We can choose to treat others with kindness and courtesy, and take our chances with how they feel about us.

"Other people are all critical and judgmental." This self-defeating attitude often accompanies the one immediately above, and is at the core of most social anxiety. So, even though we falsely believe that it is essential to please others, it is very unlikely we will. No wonder we're anxious! Are there critical and judgmental people in the world? Of course. But is it helpful to assume that everyone is that way? Again, it's best to assume people are neutral until we can clear evidence otherwise.

"I have to control my thoughts. Bad thoughts make me a bad person!" This is a kind of mental and emotional perfectionism. The truth is that thoughts come and go and it's very unlikely we can completely control our thinking process. We can only control how we respond to our thoughts. Likewise, even the most morally upright people have negative thoughts. Trying too hard not to think something almost guarantees that we will think it. Yes, our thoughts are important, but no one thought defines who we are.

THE MINDFUL WAY TO DEAL WITH ANTS AND HIDDEN ASSUMPTIONS

If someone says to you, "You're a unicorn," how would you respond? Clearly, you wouldn't take the idea seriously. It would pass through your mind, you'd have a good laugh, and the thought would pass.

Let's say that you say to repeat to yourself, "I'm a unicorn. I'm a unicorn. I'm a unicorn." 50 times. The more you say it, the more absurd it would be. Saying "I'm a unicorn" doesn't make you one. It is fairly easy to let go of that thought.

However, there are many thoughts that are more difficult to dismiss. Some examples would be obvious negative hidden assumptions like:

"I'm a loser."

"I couldn't possibly do that."

"Nothing ever works out for me."

"People can't be trusted."

"I can't stand being rejected."

"These panic attacks are going to kill me."

"If I don't worry, something bad will happen."

We are more likely to take thoughts like these seriously. However, does having the thought mean that it is true? Or is it just a thought that happens to be passing through our mind at the moment?

If a client says to himself, "I'm a loser," does that mean that he is a "loser?" What is a loser anyway? Does that mean that he is completely incompetent at everything he does? Or is that just a thought that is passing through his mind because he is struggling with a difficult situation?

Think about your own thoughts. Let's say you are driving through heavy traffic and someone cuts in front of you. In that instance, your mind is likely to slap a negative label on the other driver. But does that make it so? If you got to know that person, you might like him a lot.

Even our thoughts about ourselves can shift from moment to moment. Perhaps you are struggling with a difficult client and making no progress. Perhaps the thought will pass through your mind, "I'm not very good at this therapy stuff." But two clients later, all is going smoothly, so your thought is "Wow, I'm really good at this."

The basic goal of mindfulness-based therapies is to be aware of our inner life (thoughts, feelings, physical sensations) without being too entangled with it. Thoughts, feelings, and physical sensations come and go. They are data that we can use if they are helpful but can let go of if they are not.

In their outstanding workbook on mindfulness, *The Mindfulness and Acceptance Workbook for Anxiety*, Dr. John Forsyth and Georg Eifert have described three metaphors that encourage clients to develop a more neutral and accepting stance towards their inner experience. In her book *Freeing Yourself from Anxiety*, Dr. Tamar Chansky also described similar methods to encourage a calmer and more accepting approach to our thoughts and feelings. The essence of these approaches are described in Handout 6-H.

HANDOUT 6-H
MINDFUL ACCEPTANCE OF THOUGHTS AND FEELINGS

You have learned that many of our most distressing feelings are caused by Automatic Negative Thoughts (ANTS). You have also learned that ANTS are an inevitable part of life, and they will come and go no matter what we do.

The key to emotional well-being is to change how we *interpret* our ANTS. Do we view them as absolute truth, or are they just passing experiences that we can use or let go of as we see fit?

Practitioners of Acceptance and Commitment Therapy (ACT) have used metaphors to describe this ability to step back and get a more detached and realistic response to our inner experiences. Here are a few:

1. Imagine that you are a movie screen. Over time images are projected on you. Some of the images are happy, some scary, some sad, and some angry. The images come and go. However, you are the screen. You have a value-based self that can observe these thoughts and feelings as they occur. You are mindful of them but they do not define you. You are not your thoughts and feelings. You are the place and space where thoughts and feelings occur.

2. Imagine that you are a chessboard. There is a game of chess being played on you between your negative and positive thoughts. Your thoughts are doing battle, but you are the board. You're indifferent; you don't care which side wins or loses. You are not your thoughts and feelings. You are the place and space where your thoughts and feelings occur.

3. You are watching TV. Images and sounds come and go. You are aware of the images but you recognize that they are all "on TV" and not necessarily reality. You can use your intelligence and values to help you determine what information needs to be taken seriously and what can be let go. There might be a commercial that has a very emotional message such as "Don't miss this once in a lifetime opportunity!" In spite of the urgency of the commercial, you know that it's "just a commercial," so you let it pass. No matter what is on the TV (news, sports, entertainment), you are the ultimate authority on what you do with the information that is presented. And if the information is not useful, you just let it pass.

4. Try to imagine the wisest person you can think of—someone who remains calm and thoughtful through any storm; someone who is accepting and compassionate in all situations. Perhaps it is a relative or loved one. Perhaps it is a religious figure such as Jesus or the Buddha. Perhaps you can even form a "committee" of several wise, thoughtful, and compassionate individuals. As your thoughts and feelings pass through your awareness, imagine this wise person (or committee) speaking to you. The person or committee does not criticize or judge you for your passing thoughts and feelings, and is able to provide some wise perspective on your situation. As best you can, imagine what this person or committee has to say to you.

Chapter Seven: The Behavioral Component

At the beginning of my seminars, I always ask the participants to raise their hands if they have ever felt anxiety. Everyone chuckles and raises their hands. I then pose the question: "If anxiety is a universal human experience, why do we sometimes call it a 'disorder'?" Perhaps anxiety itself is not the problem. Maybe the real problem is that we so dislike feeling anxious that we will do almost anything to avoid it. That is the key word: AVOIDANCE. We might avoid situations (e.g., social events, bridges, air travel). We might avoid certain thoughts (e.g., vainly trying to resist troubling thoughts), or we might try to avoid physical sensations that we deem to be unpleasant (e.g., taking a beta blocker so we won't experience rapid heartbeat).

If a situation is really dangerous or seems immoral to us, then avoiding it would make great sense. However, so many things that we avoid might be worthwhile or even pleasant if we could just get ourselves to do them. After a long history of avoiding social events, you might actually enjoy them if you gave them a try. Likewise, after a long history of avoiding air travel, you might find the freedom to travel to any destination will open the door to life experiences that you never thought possible.

Not only does avoidance keep us from enjoying life as fully as we might, it is not an effective strategy. The more we avoid something, the more our mind will see it as threatening or dangerous. It reinforces the idea that anxiety is intolerable and we are not capable of managing it effectively. To be truly free and to reach our goals, we need to not allow anxiety to keep us from doing those worthwhile things that we want to do.

To illustrate how easy it is to develop a pattern of avoidance, I love to tell my clients about the famous "neurotic" mouse experiment. It involved constructing a two-room mouse apartment with a white room and a black room. The mouse was placed in the black room and an electric shock was administered through the floor. If the mouse happened to run to the white room, the shock was turned off and the mouse was never shocked again. If the mouse was picked up and placed back into the black room, he would immediately escape into the white room. In fact, if the mouse was repeatedly returned to the black room, he would go back to the white room as soon as possible.

To understand why this is happening, we all have to return to psychology 101 when we learned about Ivan Pavlov and classical conditioning. We know that if a neutral stimulus is paired with an aversive stimulus, the neutral stimulus likewise becomes aversive. So when the mouse is placed in the black room, he will naturally respond with fear. He can't help it; it's a conditioned response, and he doesn't stick around long enough to habituate to the black room. In addition, it might be assumed that the reduction in fear that the mouse experiences when he runs into the white room might serve as a positive reinforcement for his behavior. Now we have operant conditioning à la B. F. Skinner, in which any behavior that is rewarded tends to be repeated.

If we were the mouse, we would probably do the same thing and we would consider ourselves pretty wise in doing so. Why hang out somewhere when you can feel more comfortable somewhere else? We all have our "black room" of thoughts, feelings, and situations that we avoid.

Now if our "black room" is indeed dangerous, impulsive, foolish, or immoral, then it makes sense not to go there. But what if the "black room" has a lot to offer and would help us live out an important value? We would be missing out.

Let's suppose that we close the door of the black room so the mouse can't escape. We fill the room with food, mouse companionship, and other things that a mouse would love. Then we put the mouse back in the black room. Of course, he will be afraid at first, but eventually his fear will abate and he will be able to enjoy all the room has to offer.

Clients enjoy hearing about the "neurotic" mouse and find it helpful in understanding their own patterns of avoidance. Handout 7-A presents a client-version of the experiment.

HANDOUT 7-A
THE NEUROTIC MOUSE EXPERIMENT

Chances are, you have developed a pattern of avoiding situations that make you anxious. If you feel panicky on an airplane, you probably won't fly. If you are terrified of social events, you probably avoid them if you can. On the surface, it clearly makes sense to avoid what makes you feel uncomfortable. However, we now understand that avoiding anxiety-producing situations leads to a greater level of anxiety in the end. Besides, avoidance might cause us to miss out on something that we would dearly like to do.

To show you how easy it is to develop a pattern of avoidance, I want to tell you about the famous "neurotic mouse" experiment. A two-room mouse "apartment" was constructed. One room was white and the other was black. A mouse was placed in the black room and administered a painful but harmless electric shock through the floor. The mouse would initially freeze but would eventually start running around in an apparent effort to escape the shock. Let's say that just by chance, he runs into the white room. At that point, the electricity is turned off and he is never shocked again.

If you pick the mouse up and place him back into the black room, he is likely to run to the white. Place him back in the black again and again, and he will continue to escape to the white room, even though he is never shocked again.

The mouse has developed a conditioned respond to the black room. Put him in there, and he immediately feels afraid. He can't help it, and he never stays in the black room long enough to learn that he is safe there. Also, when he goes into the white room, he experiences a reduction in anxiety, which likely feels good to him. Since it always feels good to run into the white room, he will do it every time.

Now if the black room were indeed dangerous, the mouse's behavior would be appropriate. However, we know that he is equally safe in both rooms. Unfortunately, the mouse won't know he is safe until he spends some time there.

Let's suppose that we close the door, and place some mouse food and another mouse companion in the black room. When we again place the mouse in the black room, he will initially feel quite afraid. However, since there is no way out, his fear will eventually dissipate. He might even decide that the black room is preferable.

To overcome your fear, you might also have to go into the black room. Fortunately, you don't have to do it all at once. You can do it in little steps. Your therapist will help you learn how to do this.

CONFRONTING FEARS

If people are going to overcome their fears, they will have to step into whatever their "black room" is. They don't have to do it all at once; taking small steps often is the best approach. To help clients confront their fears in small steps we teach them to measure their level of anxiety using Subjective Units of Distress, or SUDS. At any point in time, we are someplace on a line between 1 and 100 SUDS. One SUD represents absolute peace and tranquility. One hundred SUDS would be you are tied to the railroad tracks and a train is coming. Seventy-five SUDS would be bad enough that you would avoid it if possible. Fifty SUDS would be very uncomfortable but you would do it if necessary.

Encourage your clients to identify situations that trigger anxiety and avoidance. Ask them to indicate how many SUDS they would experience if they were confronted with that situation. Sometimes they will have a difficult time finding anything less than 90–100 SUDS. You can help them identify situations that trigger more moderate SUDS by asking thoughtful questions. For example, if someone with social anxiety would experience 100 SUDS if he had to speak to a group of strangers, you might ask him how many SUDS he would experience if he knew the people and only had to talk for a minute about something he knows well. Chances are he will give that a lower SUDS level. Clients can use Handout 7-B to measure their own anxiety levels.

HANDOUT 7-B
MEASURING ANXIETY: HOW MANY SUDS DO YOU HAVE?

The key to overcoming anxiety is to confront your feared situations in small steps. To help with this, psychologists have invented the SUDS scale to measure anxiety. SUDS stands for Subjective Units of Distress. At any point in time, our level of distress is somewhere between 1 and 100 SUDS. One SUD represents absolute peace and tranquility (which probably doesn't happen in real life), and 100 SUDS represents the highest level of terror you could imagine (e.g., you're tied to a railroad track and the train is coming).

Think about some of the situations that you fear and ask yourself how many SUDS you would feel if you had to confront that situation. For example, if you avoid public speaking, how many SUDS would you feel if you had to do it? How many SUDS do you feel just THINKING about doing it? Try to find things that would trigger different levels of SUDS: high, moderate, or low.

For example:

Speaking to a group of 10 or more people and I do not know any of them (100 SUDS)

Speaking to executives and managers in my company who are higher on the corporate ladder (100 SUDS)

Talking to a group of 10 or more of my co-workers (85 SUDS)

Speaking to a smaller group of co-workers on a subject that I know very well (75 SUDS)

Talking to close relatives at a family reunion (50 SUDS)

Now think about what you fear and try to find situations that would fit in the following categories.

90–100 SUDS

80–89 SUDS

70–79 SUDS

60–69 SUDS

50–59 SUDS

Below 50 SUDS

DEVELOPING COURAGE

Of course, many clients will be reluctant to confront their fears. As therapists, we must honor and respect their hesitation. If confronting their fears was easy, they would have done it on their own without pursuing therapy. We must also honor their autonomy and freedom not to confront any fear that they feel is just too great. Therapists should use the principles of Motivational Interviewing to help clients develop their own intrinsic motivation. We cannot supply the motivation for them.

In order to encourage clients to confront their fears, I love to ask the following question: "When in the past did you do something that was very scary at first, but after a while it wasn't so bad? Maybe you even learned to enjoy it."

What you will find is that we all have overcome a fear at some time or other. We learned to ride a bicycle, drive a car, or play a musical instrument. We moved to a new community, attended a new school, or started a new job. The only reason that I can now present my seminars to hundreds of professionals at a time is because my first job after college was teaching high school. If I could stand in front of hostile teens, I felt I could stand in front of anyone!

When taking a client's history, we need to look for negative factors such as abuse, trauma, or dysfunctional families. However, we also need to explore a client's triumphs, successes, and fears that they have been able to overcome.

When we think about anxiety this way, it takes on a different meaning. Rather than being all bad, it can actually be a sign that we are growing. If we decide to take on a new worthwhile challenge or pursue a new opportunity, we will undoubtedly leave our comfort zone and experience some anxiety. By pushing through this kind of anxiety, we can often accomplish more than we thought possible.

You can give Handout 7-C to clients to help them identify fears that they have already overcome.

HANDOUT 7-C
WHAT FEARS HAVE YOU ALREADY OVERCOME?

Everyone has overcome fears in their lives. You have too! You learned how to ride a bicycle or drive a car. You started participating in a sport or learned to play a musical instrument. You took a class in school that seemed overwhelming at first. Perhaps you started a new relationship, moved to a new city, or started a new job.

Think back about anything in your life that was very scary or uncomfortable at first, but eventually become a lot easier with time. Maybe you even began to enjoy it.

What was your initial fear?

_____

_____

_____

How did you cope with that fear?

_____

_____

_____

How do you feel now about what you were able to do?

_____

_____

_____

THE MINDFUL APPROACH TO CONFRONTING FEARS

The practitioners of ACT would agree that we want to encourage clients to confront their fears, but only if the fear is getting in the way of their living their lives to the fullest. There is no need to confront a fear just for the sake of confronting it. But if clients believe that their fears are keeping them from living out important values, then we might want to encourage them to confront them.

As already noted, ACT is a behavioral-based therapy in that the focus is on what we choose to do with our hands, feet, and mouth. Thoughts and feelings come and go, but we want to make behavioral choices on our value-based commitment that we have made to self and others. It is not being anxiety free; it's living life to the fullest in spite of anxiety or other negative feelings.

In their book, *The Mindfulness and Acceptance Workbook for Anxiety*, Forsyth and Eifert describe two lovely metaphors that illustrate the idea of making value-based decisions in spite of negative thoughts and feelings. These metaphors are described in Handout 7-D.

HANDOUT 7-D
MAKING VALUE-BASED DECISIONS IN SPITE OF NEGATIVE THOUGHTS AND FEELINGS: TWO HELPFUL METAPHORS

(Adapted from *The Mindfulness and Acceptance Workbook for Anxiety* by Forsythe and Eifert)

"Your life is waiting for you."

Imagine that you are walking down the road of life. Ahead of you lie all your goals and aspirations. Suddenly, there is a sign blocking your way. The sign is loaded with negative messages such as "You don't deserve success," "You better not try this because it would be humiliating to fail," and "What makes you think you can do this?"

At this point, you have a choice. You might decide that you must somehow overcome the sign before moving on. So, you try to figure out what the sign means. You might try to explore what life experiences have caused your sign to say what it does. Or you might take a drug, so you can't even read the sign.

But another alternative would be to just pick up the sign and take it with you. In other words, don't try to overcome your anxiety. Don't try to figure it out. Just take your anxiety with you. Allow yourself to feel the anxiety but don't let it keep you from moving ahead in life and striving to reach worthwhile goals.

"Keep driving the bus."

You are a bus driver heading down the road of life. Ahead of you are your valued goals and aspirations. As you drive along, passengers get on and off. Some of the passengers will be positive and encouraging ("Go for it! You've got what it takes."). Many will be neutral. But some will be negative and discouraging ("You can't do this, you better give up.").

At this point, you have a choice. You could stop the bus and attempt to silence the negative passengers. Perhaps you will argue with them or even beg them to be quiet. Maybe they agree to be quiet, but in return they want to decide where the bus goes. In other words, your negative thoughts and feelings have hijacked your life and are steering you away from those things that matter most to you.

Your other alternative is to make no effort to argue with, overcome, or silence the negative passengers. Instead, you let them say whatever they want, but you don't allow them to dictate where you drive the bus. Negative thoughts and feelings come and go but you are in the driver's seat and you keep the bus headed in the direction of your goals.

VALUE-BASED LIVING

If clients want to make more value-based decisions in their lives, it only makes sense to help them determine what their values are. So spending some time in values clarification can be an important aspect of therapy. To help clients with this, you can suggest the following exercise:

"Imagine it is your 85th birthday, and everyone who cares about you has gathered to honor you on that great occasion. What would you want them to say about you? How did you impact their lives? What contributions did you make? What did you achieve?" You can use Handout 7-E to present this idea to clients.

HANDOUT 7-E
WHAT ARE YOUR VALUES?

As you learn to confront your fears, you will be able to make more decisions based on your values rather than the negative feeling of the moment. Thus, it makes sense to spend some time getting clear on what some of your values are. Here is an exercise that you might find helpful.

Imagine that it is your 85th birthday and everyone who cares for you has gathered to honor you on your special day. Ask yourself the following questions:

What would I want them to say about me?

_____

_____

_____

What contributions did I make?

_____

_____

_____

How did I add value to their lives?

_____

_____

_____

What worthwhile things did I achieve?

_____

_____

_____

What personal qualities did they admire most?

_____

_____

_____

VALUE-BASED VS. EMOTIONALLY BASED DECISIONS

Human beings have a tendency to make decisions based on emotion. There are many times when that is certainly OK. For example, I hug my wife because I feel loving toward her or I listen to a certain song because it makes me happy. Most everyone would agree that those are good choices.

However, there are times when making decisions based on pure emotions might not be helpful or productive. For example, a client might say, "I didn't go to work yesterday because I was so depressed." As therapists, we understand that depression is associated with high fatigue, low energy, loss of interest, and feelings of hopelessness. These certainly make going to work more difficult, but is depression itself a reason not to go to work? Many depressed people go to work because going to work is more important than how they feel at the moment.

I sometimes encourage my clients to try this exercise. I suggest that as they go through their day, they should take note of decisions they make and try to determine whether each decision was primarily based on emotion or on values. Of course, this might not always be easy to figure out. Sometimes feelings conflict, values conflict, or values and feelings might agree. I just encourage them to do the best they can. Clients can use Handout 7-F to help them with this exercise.

As you go through your day, take note of decisions you make. Try to determine if you based each decision primarily on the immediate emotion or if it was based on your values. Sometimes it won't be completely clear how you made the decision. Sometimes emotions and values agree and sometimes there can be competing values in play. Nevertheless, do the best you can to determine what led to your decision. Use this chart to help you keep track of your decisions. I have included two examples to help you get started.

Examples:

Decision	Emotion-based	Value-based
Felt depressed but went to work		X
Ate unhealthy food for lunch	X	

Now you record your decisions:

Decision	Emotion-based	Value-based

In summary, both CBT and ACT approaches to therapy advocate helping clients confront their fears. Each particular anxiety disorder poses its own behavioral challenges, which will be reviewed when we discuss each specific disorder.

Chapter Eight:
Treating Panic Disorder and Agoraphobia

There are few things more frightening than a severe panic attack; particularly if it is your first and you do not understand what is happening. However, in reviewing the symptoms of a panic attack, we learn a lot about how to help our clients. First, we have to understand the difference between a panic attack and panic disorder. A panic attack is a discrete event that either occurs "out of the blue" or in certain situations. Panic attacks can occur in the context of other anxiety disorders such as social anxiety disorder. If we review the symptoms of a panic attack, we see the following physical symptoms listed:

1. Rapid heartbeat
2. Difficulty breathing or a feeling of choking or being smothered
3. Sweating
4. Trembling or shaking
5. Feeling dizzy or faint
6. Tingling or numbness in extremities
7. Digestive distress

If you think back to Chapter Five, which dealt with the physiological component of anxiety, you no doubt recognize these symptoms. The emergency response system has been triggered when it isn't needed. The body is trying to protect you from a perceived danger that isn't there. It is a false alarm.

Even though these physical sensations are harmless, we have a long human history of associating them with danger. So in response to these physical symptoms, the mind begins to generate catastrophic thoughts. Thus, the psychological symptoms of panic include:

1. Fear of dying
2. Fear of going crazy or losing control

These catastrophic thoughts trigger more physical discomfort, which triggers more catastrophic thoughts, and so on. We call this the panic cycle.

We do not always know why someone has the first panic attack, nor do we really need to know. Some individuals are more genetically predisposed to attacks, and panic attacks often get started when the individual is going through a period of intense stress. However, I have seen situations in which the first panic attack was triggered by a negative reaction to medication. I have seen food allergies or food poisoning trigger attacks. This suggests that we don't want to attribute too much meaning to panic attacks or suggest that they are signs of a deeper psychopathology. When you review a client's history, you might not find the early life issues or trauma that we often see in clients with other conditions. Of course they might be there, but, but then again they might not.

Suppose a business executive is attending an important lunch meeting. There is a lot riding on the meeting so he is feeling tense. The food doesn't agree with him and the room is warm. Out of the blue, he notices that his heart is beating fast, he has trouble catching a breath, he is having cold sweats, and his hands are shaking. He immediately assumes that he is having a medical emergency—probably a heart attack. Of course, these scary thoughts only make his physical sensations stronger and increase his fear. His colleagues take him to the emergency room where he is thoroughly checked out, and there is no sign of a heart attack or other serious medical problems. He is told that it was probably a panic attack and is sent on his way.

If that was the end of it, all would be well. Unfortunately, the episode was so frightening that our executive cannot help but worry about it. He is bound to think, "I wonder if I really have a medical problem that they couldn't find. Maybe I am really on the verge of a mental breakdown. I better be careful and make sure that doesn't happen to me again."

At this point, the panic attack has morphed into the condition we call Panic Disorder. This disorder includes the occurrence of attacks plus

1. Persistent worry about having more attacks
2. Worry about the implications of the attacks (e.g., "Something must be terribly wrong with me.")
3. Change in behavior to avoid attacks ("I won't go to that restaurant again. I've got to avoid getting myself riled up.")

The mind has a kind of evil logic that says, "Where would an attack be dangerous or embarrassing? What are the situations where it is difficult to exit from where you are? So a number of situations become triggers for fear and are thus avoided (e.g., being home by yourself, being away from home, large crowds, sitting in the middle seat in a row, public transportation, bridges and overpasses, having an enclosed MRI done, or sitting in a dentist chair). This is what we call Panic Disorder with Agoraphobia.

Agoraphobia is not so much a fear of the place per se. It is the fear of the feelings that you will have in the place. In other words, it is the fear that you will panic.

In my own practice, I have seen clients who have had hundreds of attacks and others who have had only one or two. In some cases, the people with only a couple attacks have been more disabled than those who have had many. The problem is that they are so afraid of having more attacks that they have organized their lives around their fears and avoid any situation that has even the slightest chance of triggering an attack. Individuals who have had many attacks are at least trying to confront feared situations and have learned that every panic attack, no matter how bad, eventually ends.

TREATMENT OF PANIC DISORDER

Clients will want to describe their attack(s) to you in great detail. As a therapist, it is easy to have an "I've heard all this before" attitude. However, clients will feel like no one else has ever felt anything like this, so the unique aspects of their experience should be acknowledged. Once clients feel that you empathize with their suffering, you can get down to the process of treatment itself. The treatment of panic disorder is not always easy, but it is fairly straightforward and follows four basic steps: education, physiological interventions, cognitive interventions, and behavioral interventions.

Education: It is essential that clients develop a complete understanding of what is going on with them. Often they hold catastrophic but inaccurate beliefs such as "This could kill me." "I might be going crazy." "Panic attacks are so awful and dangerous that I must do everything I can to prevent them."

Therapists need to devote considerable time sharing the facts about panic. I always use the "Mr. Caveman goes for a walk," story to describe the emergency response system. I explain that these unpleasant physical sensations are actually the body's way of protecting them from a perceived threat. These reactions are harmless, time-limited, and much like what goes on when you're excited, angry, or exercising.

At all times, this teaching process should be done in an interactive conversational style. The therapist shouldn't read off facts in a rote manner. Instead, the therapist should continually check in with clients to see if the information is making sense to them (e.g., "How does this sound to you?" "How do you relate this to your own experience?" "Does this information ring true to you, or is it too hard to believe?").

Clients will process this information in different ways. On rare occasions, this corrective information is enough in itself. Reassured that their reactions are normal, they no longer fear panic and so are well on their way to complete recovery.

More often, however, clients will be doubtful. The facts you share with them are so contrary to their subjective experience that they will have a hard time believing them (e.g., "Rationally, I know what you say is true; but I just can't believe it at the moment. I'm just so panicky."). Therapists should not be put off by this skepticism and clients' doubts and worries should be acknowledged and affirmed (e.g., "I know that these ideas might be difficult to believe." "It's OK not to be sure about this. How do you feel about going ahead with treatment and seeing if these ideas ring true to you later on?").

Physiological Interventions: Clients will benefit from applying the trio of body calming methods described in Chapter Five. Probably *deep abdominal breathing* is the most powerful. Remember, it is important to help clients learn the mechanics of abdominal breathing and then encourage them to practice about 8–10 times a day. They need to practice when they are feeling OK and not wait until they are on the verge of a panic attack. When they practice regularly, they develop a body memory for how it feels, which makes it more likely that breathing will be helpful to them when they begin to panic.

Likewise, the other two techniques, *progressive relaxation* and *visualization*, can be helpful to clients. Although muscle relaxation might be difficult to employ in a crisis, clients who have practiced it regularly are often able to maintain a higher level of comfort. Also, if clients have a menu of pleasant scenes, images, memories, or ideas handy, they can often use them to help them feel more relaxed. The trio of body-calming techniques can be seen in Handout 5-C in Chapter 5.

As helpful as these techniques can be, it is important to remember that we do not want to make "feeling relaxed" the ultimate goal of treatment. We don't want clients to struggle and fight to become calm and feel like failures if they can't. That is obviously counterproductive.

Remember that our ultimate goal is not to relax, but to be OK even when the body is not relaxed. The real goal is to experience and accept these physical sensations as normal and benign reactions. It involves trusting the body and letting it do what it is going to do.

The technique *interoceptive exposure* helps clients develop the ability to tolerate and accept high levels of physiological arousal. As mentioned in Chapter Five, this technique involves encouraging clients to willingly experience these sensations in a safe environment. So clients who fear rapid heart rate can be coached to run in place, walk on a treadmill, go jogging, or climb stairs in order to get their heart beating fast. If possible, they could do some of this in session and then do it at home.

For clients who do not like to feel like they do not have enough air, they can practice holding their breaths or breathing through a soda straw. I sometimes have breath-holding contests with my clients. I once had a client whose fear was that her throat would close up during a panic attack. I suggested that we both try to close our throats for as long as we can. We both strained to close our throats but soon found that it was impossible to do so. A description of interoceptive exposure techniques can be found in Handout 5-D in Chapter Five.

Practitioners of mindfulness-based therapies such as ACT would agree that we do not want to struggle to calm the body. They would advocate the stance of learning to embrace whatever the body happens to be doing at the moment. There is no need to avoid the feelings or judge yourself for how you feel. You can just accept it with an attitude of kindness and compassion. If you listen to a typical guided mindfulness meditation, there is no mention of "relaxing" or "getting calm." Instead, the goal is to be consciously aware of whatever you are experiencing. Of course, this often leads to a state of relaxation, but that is a byproduct of the technique and not its goal. Some simple mindfulness meditations can be found in Handout 5-F in Chapter Five.

Cognitive Interventions: The emotional intensity of a panic attack is so strong that it is difficult to see how anything "cognitive" can be of much help. Clients will often say, "Yes, I know that I'm not in danger, but it feels so real in the moment." Nevertheless, helping clients develop a more realistic appraisal of what is going on can be quite helpful. At least, it gives the "rational" mind some ammunition to counteract what their emotions are telling them.

The process for determining a client's Automatic Negative Thoughts (ANTS) in a panic attack is essentially the same as any other anxiety issues. That is, clients are simply asked to identify what thoughts are going through their mind during an attack. Often they will say, "I'm not thinking anything. I'm just so frightened." As a therapist, your response should be to acknowledge and accept these responses as being absolutely true in the client's experience. You can then go on to say, "Yes, it definitely is difficult to notice what your thoughts are in an attack. However, research suggests that we are always talking to ourselves in our minds and commenting on what is going on with us. Let's see if we can figure out what you are saying to yourself in that moment."

Clients' reactions to this inquiry will vary. Some will have thoughts that comment on the intensity of their distress, such as, "I can't stand this," or "I've got to get out of here." Other thoughts will be catastrophic appraisals of what is happening. "This really might be a heart attack." "I am completely out of control." "I'm going crazy."

Once clients have identified their catastrophic thoughts, you ask permission to ask questions that might help them develop more helpful thoughts. Typical questions might be "Aside from how you feel, what is the evidence that you're dying?" "If you had to feel this way to save the life of a loved one, could you do it?" "How many of your attacks eventually ended?"

Based on these questions and what the client has learned from the facts covered during the educational phase, you help the client develop a handful of coping statements. These statements should provide a more rational and realistic appraisal of the situation. Typical coping statements might include, "This feels terrible, but I know I'm safe." "My mind says that I need to escape, but I'm as safe here as anywhere." "It feels like it will go on forever, but they always pass." "I know that this is a lot like being excited or exercising." "I can practice my breathing and ride this out until it passes."

Notice that the statements are fairly realistic and acknowledge the person's distress. Overly positive statements such as "I will stay serene and calm through it all," are not helpful because they deny the reality of how the person is feeling.

Once you have helped clients develop their coping statements, encourage them to write them down on index cards or load them into their electronic device so they can review them regularly. If possible, they should memorize them. These statements will come in handy as a "reality check" when they begin to panic. Clients can use Handout 8-A to help them develop their coping statements.

HANDOUT 8-A
COPING STATEMENTS FOR PANIC

What catastrophic thoughts do you have? (e.g., "I can't stand this." "I'm in danger." "I'm dying." "This might be a heart attack.")

What are some facts that you can use to counteract your catastrophic thoughts? (e.g., "These responses are normal." "Your body is trying to protect you." "These responses are a lot like being excited, angry, or exercising.")

What questions can you ask yourself to counteract these catastrophic thoughts? (e.g., "How many of your past attacks have eventually ended?" "If you had to feel this way to save the life of a loved one, would you do it?")

Write a list of coping statements to help you cope with a panic attack. (e.g., "This feels bad, but I know I'm safe." "I can practice my breathing until it passes."

There is a powerful technique for panic attacks that has both cognitive and behavioral aspects called the *experimental method*. The purpose of this technique is to help clients test the validity of their fears in the moment in order to be assured that their fears are unfounded. Sometimes the fear feels so "real" in the moment that it is extremely difficult to question its validity. One way to help with this is to do something in the moment that helps individuals believe that they are more in control that they might think.

For example, suppose a person fears rapid heartbeat because they can't shake the thought that "This really is a heart attack this time!" If the client has been checked out medically and no heart problem detected, you could ask, "If you were really having a heart attack, would you be able to jog in place?" The client will likely tell you that they probably could not. If so, you might suggest that when they feel an attack, they should start jogging in place. The fact that they can do this without collapsing or doubling over in pain can be a reassurance that their fear is false.

Likewise, if a person feels that they "can't control their breathing," they might be encouraged to immediately begin deep abdominal breathing or even hold their breath. Again, this will show them that they have more control in the situation than they realize.

The experimental method might also involve "mental" tests such as "If I was going crazy, could I sing my favorite song? Could I count the ceiling tiles or light fixtures in the room? Could I silently recite my favorite poem, affirmation, or prayer to myself?" As clients perform these actions in the moment, they develop increased confidence that their biggest fears are unfounded. Handout 8-B can be used to help clients develop experiments that they can employ if they feel a panic attack coming on.

What catastrophic fears do you have in a panic attack? (e.g., "I'm dying!" "I'm losing control!")

What behavioral or mental experiments can you conduct in the moment to test the validity of your fears? ("Can I jog in place?" "Can I hold my breath?" "Can I count to 100 by 5's?" "Can I recite the Pledge of Allegiance?")

Behavioral Interventions: True to the "Three C's" model of all anxiety problems, clients will eventually need to confront their fears. They should be encouraged to gradually approach situations that they may have been avoiding. If they have been avoiding large crowds or shopping malls, they should be encouraged to place themselves in these situations a little bit at a time. For example, a client could go to the shopping mall for 5 minutes, then for 10, then for 20, 30, and so on. Perhaps the client could begin by going on a day when there might be few people in the mall and later go at times when there is likely to be a large crowd. One of my clients wanted to attend a full hour-long church service but was not ready to do it all at once. So we got the church bulletin to determine when it might be appropriate for her to leave (e.g., as the congregation was rising to sing a hymn). Doing it this way, she was eventually able to sit through the whole service.

A person who has been avoiding the local subway might ride it from station A to station B with a friend. Then the person might ride from station A to station C with a friend, and then start riding by themselves.

A person with severe agoraphobia who has been housebound for some time might begin by just walking to the end of their own driveway. Then they can walk by a neighbor's house, then two neighbors' houses, and so on.

Of course, this can be quite scary for clients so we need to take their fears seriously and not push them to do what they are not ready to do. They might want someone with them at first but then tackle the situation on their own. They should be encouraged to hang in there and embrace the fear as much as they can. If they must retreat they can do so, but they should be encouraged to place themselves back into the situation as much as possible.

A nice metaphor to share with clients is to imagine they are a bird such as a seagull or pelican who is floating on the ocean's surface. As waves come, the bird just rides each wave up and down. The bird doesn't fly away from the wave. He lets the wave come to him and he just rides it out. In such a way, clients can be encouraged to ride the panic wave up and down and not try to escape it. The paradox is that if they are willing to feel some panic, they will likely have fewer attacks and won't be overly distressed by the ones that they have. However, if they are completely unwilling to risk attacks, then panic will be a greater problem. Clients can use Handout 8-C to help them develop a plan for confronting situations that trigger panic.

One of my favorite clients of all time was a woman in her early 50s who was convinced that she was "falling apart" at the outset of therapy. One of her symptoms was that she was afraid to climb stairs. If she went up one or two steps, she would immediately feel that her heart rate was accelerating. Since it takes more effort to go up steps, it would be expected that the heart rate might go up a bit. Most of us wouldn't even notice the change. However, she was so tuned into her body that the heart rate increase frightened her and led her to panic. She would cope with this by sitting down on the steps for a few minutes before collecting herself and going up a couple more steps. It would take her about an hour to go up a standard flight of stairs. Fortunately, she was an excellent candidate for CBT and she responded beautifully. After about six weeks, she was climbing stairs normally and doing a number of things she had been avoiding (e.g., going driving with her husband).

OVERCOMING PANIC BY CONFRONTING FEARED SITUATIONS

List situations that you are now avoiding and give them an estimated SUDS rating (e.g., going to the mall for an hour, 95 SUDS; going to the mall for 30 minutes, 80 SUDS; going to the mall for 15 minutes, 55 SUDS).

Based on your SUDS ratings, decide what situations you will confront first. Write them in the space below.

After you have successfully confronted these low SUDS situations, what SUDS situations will you confront next?

What high SUDS situations will you confront when you are ready?

List the tools you will use to help you confront your fears (e.g., breathing, coping statements, experimental method, etc.).

Remember, when confronting a feared situation, try to hang in there the best you can. If you must retreat, do so, but try to put yourself back into the situation as soon as possible. Imagine that you are a seagull out on the ocean, riding up and down as waves come and go but not flying away from them.

Chapter Nine: Treating the Fear of Flying

In the twenty-first century, the inability to get on a plane and fly somewhere can be a severe impediment. Often career opportunities are contingent on being able to fly. An individual might pass up a great vacation opportunity or family reunion just because of being unable to get on an airplane. I once worked with a woman who tearfully told me that she had recently missed the funeral of a much-beloved family member. She really wanted to go. She had purchased her ticket and packed her bag. However, when it became time to leave for the airport, she sat down at the kitchen table, burst into tears, and told her husband to go ahead without her. It was this painful experience that motivated her to seek help.

When I first started working with people who are afraid to fly, I was surprised to see that the problem was not what I thought it was. Many people, like me, have concerns about the safety of flying. I never board an airplane without considering the possibility that the plane might crash. As we're rolling down the runway to take off, I ask myself if we're going fast enough to get airborne, and I'm relieved when we finally do.

People with my kind of fear of flying will get on planes if it is important enough to do so. However, for the person who absolutely cannot and will not get on a plane that does not seem to be the problem. The problem is not what the plane will do. The problem is what they will do. Perhaps they will "crack up" on the plane or "go crazy," or "run up and down the aisle and pound on the cockpit and beg the captain to land." In other words, they are afraid of having a panic attack.

So in 90 percent of the cases that I have seen of the fear of flying, it has actually been a variation of panic disorder with agoraphobia. If you think of it, an airplane ride can be an absolute witches' brew for panic. You are confined to a small metal tube for an extended period of time, you are strapped into your seat, and you have no way of escaping. A great recipe for panic!

The good news is that if you can treat panic, you can also treat the fear of flying, because it follows the same steps.

The first step is to provide the same educational information that you would for any panic problem. Clients will be told about the emergency response system, Mr. Caveman, and will learn that their physiological responses are normal and harmless.

Then you will employ the physiological interventions. You will use interoceptive exposure and mindfulness meditation to help clients tolerate physiological arousal. You will teach breathing, relaxation, and visualization as tools to calm the body. Since passengers are allowed to listen to recordings for most of the flight, they can listen to relaxation recordings in flight.

Cognitive interventions would include helping clients develop coping statements that they can write on an index card and take with them. They can read their card before and during the flight. Since flights often last an hour or more, their coping statements should address this fact with reassuring comments that their feelings are temporary.

Clients can use the experimental method by engaging in activities that help them feel more in control at a time when they are likely to feel out of control. For example, in response to the fear that they are "losing control," clients could respond by reading the in-flight magazine, talking to a fellow passenger, noticing items in the plane, silently reciting prayers or affirmations, or simply focusing on their destination and what they plan to do on arrival.

As you can see, these interventions are the same as those used to treat panic attacks. The problem comes with behavioral interventions, in that it is difficult to get gradual practice. Flying is pretty much an all or nothing proposition. No major airline will take you up for a 5-minute spin. If you get on a plane, you will need to stay on board for quite some time.

Also, since airplane tickets are expensive, most people will not be willing to take a lot of short flights "just for practice."

Fortunately, I have found that most people who fear flying also have other situations that they either avoid or at best endure with great discomfort. I worked with one business executive who also feared elevators. It turns out that his firm had recently relocated to the 30th floor of an office tower, so he had ample opportunity to confront that fear. As he learned to overcome that fear, he developed the courage to get on planes.

Another client avoided her local mall and the rapid transit system. In preparation for her flight, she confronted those fears. Another woman visited the dentist just days before flight and started to panic in the chair. She used her tools to get through that episode, which gave her enough courage to get on her scheduled flight.

Still another client planned to attend a big football game two weeks before his flight. He was looking forward to the game, but he had a tendency to be uncomfortable in large crowds. We worked to get him through the football game, which helped him get on the flight.

If clients do not have other situations that make them uncomfortable, you can still use the other techniques to prepare them for the flight. Then you might have them imagine a flight while they are sitting in your office. Allow them to visualize going to the airport, getting on the plane, and effectively using the tools to help them get through it.

As mentioned, in about 90 percent of the cases that I have seen, fear of flying has been a variation of panic disorder. However, there is the other 10 percent in which the fear stems entirely from safety concerns. For example, I worked with a woman who had been on a flight that experienced a sudden and severe air pocket, which made the plane fall hundreds of feet before regaining stability. Some passengers who didn't have their seatbelts fastened suffered minor injuries. My client was not hurt but was clearly traumatized by the experience. She had not been on a flight since.

When the issue concerns safety, the tools of CBT still apply. You would use all of your physiological and cognitive interventions. The only difference is that your coping statements will more directly address safety concerns (e.g., "Thousands of flights take off and land every day and crashes are extremely rare.").

I always encourage my clients to call, text, or email after they reach their destination. They love sharing their triumph with me and I enjoy hearing from them.

Chapter Ten:
Treating the Fear of Highway Driving

There are many people who find it impossible to drive on limited-access roads such as freeways, turnpikes, and interstate highways. They can usually drive on regular surface streets with little difficulty. If you are on a surface street and you begin to feel uncomfortable, it is usually easy to pull over to the side of the road or into a parking lot. However, limited-access highways pose a greater problem because it is much more difficult to get off of them.

Just like with fear of flying, most cases of "freeway phobia" are a variation of panic disorder. The fear is feeling panic, not being able to exit the highway, and possibly losing control of the car.

It is easy to recognize the extra element of danger in this particular fear. If someone loses control on an airplane, that person will be quite embarrassed but will survive. However, if someone loses control of a vehicle, someone could be killed. Therefore, it is essential the clients have faith in their ability to control the vehicle even when they are feeling panicky.

Therapists can begin instilling that confidence by asking clients to recount the episode that might have triggered their fear in the first place. Often you will hear something like "I was driving the SUV with the kids in back. There were two big trucks on both sides me. I was feeling stressed. Then all of a sudden I felt this terrible rush of heat, my hands started to shake, and I felt like I might faint."

Once you have adequately affirmed the intensity of their feelings, you should then ask them to describe exactly what they did in response to their feelings. Often you will get something like "The truck to my right moved up a bit, so I could slip in behind it. Then the next lane to the right opened up, so I pulled into it. Then I noticed that there was an exit ahead, so I got to the exit, pulled into a parking lot, and then called my husband who took me home."

In reviewing this episode with clients, you will usually find that their behavior was not as "out of control" as they thought it was. Given what they felt and believed in the moment, their behavior was intentional. Somehow they had gotten themselves to safety. Of course, when you put this out to clients, they won't necessarily agree. Maybe they pulled it together that time, but they might not be so lucky the next. Nevertheless, you have at least put forward the idea that they might be more in control than they feel.

From this point, your approach to treatment will be much like it is with other variations of panic disorder. You will educate clients on the facts of the emergency response system and the normalcy and harmlessness of panic symptoms. You will want to employ interoceptive exposure to help clients tolerate high levels of physiological arousal. They can practice deep abdominal breathing. You can help them develop coping statements to memorize and say to themselves while they are driving. One of my clients had her good friend sit in the seat next to her and read her coping statements to her while she was driving.

However, the most powerful technique is the experimental method. Remember, this is when clients are encouraged to engage in behaviors "in the moment," the purpose being to reassure them that their fears are unfounded. If someone feels that they are "losing control," they can do things that demonstrate that they are in control. For example, a client might pose the question "If I was out of control, would I be able to change the radio station or adjust the radio volume?" Then to test themselves, they change the station or adjust the volume. Perhaps they can counter the fear of losing control by engaging in some mental behavior such as counting by fives, singing a favorite song, or reciting the Pledge of Allegiance. One of my clients said that she gripped the steering wheel so tightly that she was afraid that she would veer out of control. Her experiment was to hold the steering wheel with both hands, but raise both index fingers and gently tap them against the wheel. This gave her reassurance that she could control where she steered the car.

Once clients have these tools, they need to practice. Of course, they need to take very small steps. Not far from my office is a stretch of freeway that is easy to navigate. The shoulders are wide, it has a nice grassy median, and there no tricky curves. I might suggest that a client go out on a Sunday morning when traffic is light and drive from exit A to exit B. Then they could drive from exit A to exit C. They might want to have someone in the car with them for the first few trials and then try it on their own.

One of my clients was afraid to drive on all roads. She had been driving in an ice storm and had spun out of control. She became afraid of losing control even when conditions were perfect. Her first practice was to drive in the parking lot of her apartment building. Then she drove around the block, then to the grocery store and back. She had someone with her for early trials and then practiced it by herself. Eventually, she was able to drive in any situation. This was of great benefit to her because her job was about 20 miles from her home, and she had been imposing on friends to transport her to and from work.

Chapter Eleven: Treating Social Anxiety

One of the greatest benefits of life is enjoying the company of other people. Therefore, it seems particularly sad when someone's biggest fear is other people. Social Anxiety Disorder, otherwise called Social Phobia, is one of the most prevalent anxiety disorders, affecting about six million Americans.

It is also a very heterogeneous condition in that it presents itself in a wide variety of ways. It can cause individuals to avoid social events, meetings, or other gatherings of any kind. It can be an intense discomfort in any situation in which one might be the center of attention.

It might involve extreme discomfort around bosses, teachers, or other "authorities." An intimidated employee might go to great lengths to avoid running into a superior on the job.

It can include great shame and embarrassment about "looking scared" or showing physiological indicators of anxiety such as blushing, perspiring, shakiness, or difficulty speaking.

Social anxiety can also be revealed in difficulty making phone calls, feeling conspicuous if standing in line, or an inability to return items to a store.

Bill is an accountant and IT specialist for a small company. One day Bill's boss approaches him and says, "At our staff meeting next month, I would like you to take 5 to 10 minutes to describe the new accounting software." Bill designed the software, so he is the right person to talk about it. He also knows all the people who will be listening to him. It should be easy! However, poor Bill will worry and fret the entire month prior to the meeting. He will obsess about what he is going to say and will look for a way to avoid it if possible.

Then there is Kenny, whose brother has asked him to say the toast at his wedding reception next month. Again, it sounds easy enough, but poor Kenny will be so filled with dread that he will look for a way out.

THREE STAGES OF SOCIAL ANXIETY

Individuals with social anxiety suffer in three different stages: pre-event, during event, and post-event. If they know that a social event is forthcoming they will look forward to it with great dread and foreboding. Their anxiety might be so great that they have difficulty engaging in their normal activities. They will seek a way to avoid the event if possible.

If the event cannot be avoided, they will certainly suffer during it. Sometimes they find that the anxiety actually decreases during the event. Thinking about it was far worse than actually doing it. However, in other situations their anxiety reaches such a high level that the "mind goes blank," their voice cracks, or they shows physiological signs of anxiety such as sweating or blushing. Of course, this only makes the event more of an ordeal.

Finally, after the event, socially anxious individuals often engage in a painful process of self-criticism. Typical post-event thoughts might be, "That was terrible." "I made a fool of myself." "They think I'm an idiot." "I'll never do that again!"

Therapists need to be aware of these three stages of social anxiety and be prepared to address all three.

TREATMENT INTERVENTIONS

It should not be surprising that people who struggle with social anxiety have great difficulty seeking help. They might have been contemplating treatment for years, and only finally do so when things have become desperate. Maybe they have just suffered a major embarrassment. Maybe they have a major event coming up that they cannot avoid. Perhaps they have a career opportunity that will challenge their fear. Sometimes, they need to be prodded to seek help by loved ones.

Therapists need to be especially sensitive to the enormous ambivalence that these clients will exhibit. Motivational Interviewing can be used to allow clients to explore their mixed feelings and thoughtfully weigh the pros and cons of seeking help.

Since you are the "doctor," socially anxious clients may feel intimated by you and excessively deferential. Care needs to be taken to maintain a warm and casual feel to the session. I often poke fun at myself so they won't take me too seriously.

Socially anxious clients also need to be encouraged to let you know if there is anything about the therapy experience that they do not like. It is helpful to check in with them regularly to make sure they are comfortable with what is going on. However, a client's silence should not be seen as a sure indicator that all is well. They just might be too uncomfortable to tell you what they are really feeling. So, it is important to never push these clients too hard and be aware of any nonverbal signs of discomfort.

As in the other anxiety disorders, the Three C's are relevant. The trio of physiological interventions (deep breathing, muscle relaxation, and visualization) can all be used to decrease a client's level of arousal before and during the event. Deep breathing is particularly helpful because it can be done so quickly and unobtrusively.

It should be remembered, however, that much of the physiological arousal in anxiety involves involuntary reactions, so obtaining a level of absolute control is unlikely. Instead, clients can be coached to tolerate and embrace these reactions as normal and harmless. This is where interoceptive exposure and mindfulness exercises can be helpful.

If clients continue to experience reactions such as sweating or blushing, they can be coached to develop light-hearted, matter-of-fact ways to talk to others about it. "Boy, it's hot in here. I'm sweating like a pig." "I tend to blush, so I must look as red as a beet."

COGNITIVE INTERVENTIONS: MIND READING

As always, the cognitive component of treatment involves identifying, challenging, and replacing Automatic Negative Thoughts (ANTS). In social anxiety, the predominant ANT is almost always "mind reading." In other words, we are anxious around other people because we are focusing on what they might be thinking of us. We are likely having thoughts such as, "Do these people like me? I hope they think I'm smart. I don't want them to think I'm a snob." I have worked with thousands of individuals with social anxiety and almost all have agreed that mind reading is at the core of their problems.

So if the focus is on the perceived thoughts of other people, then every social event becomes a performance in which we are trying to control the thoughts of other people. Our mission is to get them to think well of us, or at least prevent them from thinking poorly of us. Unfortunately, since we don't have control over the thoughts of others, this is a setup for anxiety.

CHANGING THE SOCIAL MISSION

If the main issue in social anxiety is the effort to control the thoughts of other people, then the antidote seems clear. Clients need to be encouraged to change their mission. The old mission of getting people to think well of them is a dead end. The new mission is to encourage the other people to think well of themselves.

This idea seems so simple and commonsense, that it almost doesn't seem worth mentioning. However, when clients can accept and deeply internalize this idea, it can be an absolute life changer. I have seen many clients who experienced a dramatic decrease in their social anxiety and a dramatically improved quality of life just by making this profound change in perspective.

This is not always an easy attitude to maintain and people are likely to have setbacks and times when they just can't seem to apply the idea. But if they learn to apply it regularly, they love it!

Personally, I find myself applying this principle. If I notice that I am anxious around other people, I remind myself that I am mind reading and immediately shift my focus on making the other people comfortable. It works every time! This concept is described in Handout 11-A.

HANDOUT 11-A
FEARED SOCIAL SITUATIONS: CHANGE YOUR MISSION

We have learned that the source of our anxiety is our Automatic Negative Thoughts (ANTS). The variety of ANT most associated with social anxiety is mind reading. That is, we are anxious around other people because we are concerned about how they might be thinking of us. ("Do I fit in?" "They think I'm an idiot." "I'm boring them." "He will be annoyed if I talk to him.")

Our concern about how others view us turns every social situation into a performance. We believe that we must make other people think well of us, or at least prevent them from thinking badly of us. In other words, we are trying to control the thoughts of other people! But, can we control the thoughts of other people? Probably not, so it's any wonder that we feel anxious.

The secret of overcoming social anxiety is to change your mission. Your old mission has been "I must make them have good thoughts about me." Your new mission should be "WHAT CAN I DO TO ENCOURAGE THEM TO FEEL GOOD ABOUT THEMSELVES?"

If you are willing to adopt and internalize this new mission, it can be a life-changing experience. I realize that this may be harder than it sounds. It will require you to let go of your pride and the need to impress others. Instead, you will need to be genuinely interested and concerned about the other person.

So how do we show this concern? It's not with insincere flattery. Instead, we show it by being interested and curious about them.

So the next time you are anxious around people, be aware that you are on the wrong mission. Let go of any desire to control their thoughts and focus on being polite and cordial to them. Your social anxiety will drop dramatically and you are more likely to have a positive social experience.

HIDDEN ASSUMPTIONS IN SOCIAL ANXIETY

As mentioned in Chapter Six, it is helpful to look for recurring patterns in the client's thinking. This often reveals certain hidden assumptions or underlying attitudes that may color how the client perceives almost any situation. Following are some hidden assumptions that are prevalent in social anxiety.

"I'm not likeable."   Socially anxious people are often very self-critical and suffer from pervasive thoughts about their inadequacy or worthlessness. These assumptions were often developed early in life and are therefore difficult to challenge and change. Exploring the early life experiences that have engendered these ideas can be helpful, but insight alone is not always enough. Clients still need to develop new ways to think in the here and now.

"Everyone else is extremely critical and looking to judge me."   Often socially anxious individuals perceive that the whole world is looking down on them and ready to judge them mercilessly if given the chance. Of course, they may have people like that in their lives now, or they might have suffered at the hands of such people in the past. Even if this hidden assumption is based on real experience, it is not particularly helpful to believe that everyone else in the world is like that. Therapy should help clients be more discerning in their perceptions of others and help them identify people in their lives who are not so critical.

"Disapproval is unbearable."   Everyone would rather win the approval of others rather than be the object of their disapproval. In social anxiety, the fear of disapproval is especially intense and often debilitating. Such individuals engage in a variety of "all or none thinking." If you dislike one thing they do, you must disapprove of them completely. There is no gray area in which they can believe that they are liked "in general" even though they may have some characteristics that the other person does not like.

"Anxiety means that I'm weak or lacking in faith."   As part of their general tendency toward self-criticism, some individuals berate themselves for their anxiety. They think of themselves as "weak." People who profess a religious belief also criticize themselves for their anxiety. They believe that they would not be anxious if they just had "more faith." Of course, this tendency toward self-criticism only adds to their misery.

"Other people must not know that I'm anxious."   Many socially anxious individuals have decided that anxiety itself is so shameful that they cannot bear the idea that other people would be able to tell. They fear that their physiological reactions such as blushing or sweating will betray them and they will be found out. They will strive to hide their anxiety from others, which only serves to make the anxiety worse.

"If one person in the group dislikes me, they must all dislike me."   For example, if a person has received some negative feedback from one member of the organization (school, professional organization, workplace, church, etc.), the person assumes that this negative opinion has been spread to the other members of the group. So, if one person disapproves of me, everyone must disapprove of me. This is sometimes called "The Wildfire Fantasy," because the person believes that the bad opinion of them has spread "like a wildfire."

MORE TECHNIQUES FOR SOCIAL ANXIETY

Feared Fantasy: This excellent tool for challenging ANTS was first identified by Dr. David Burns in his classic book, *The Feeling Good Handbook*. In this technique, you ask the client to take part in a role play that will play out a client's deepest social fears. In the role play, the therapist plays the role of the client while the client plays the role of a perceived critic. The client, in the role of the critic, is coached to be downright mean and cruel, while you will demonstrate how to respond well to criticism.

To illustrate this technique we will talk about Phillip, who had severe anxiety in a number of social situations. One such situation was walking out into his yard, because he was afraid to encounter the woman who lived next door. The reason for this was that although his yard was well kept and looked pretty good, the neighbor's yard was immaculate and perfectly maintained. His fear was that the neighbor disapproved of him because his poor yard. What would he say if she came out and spoke to him? What if she criticized him for his yard?

Here is how we did the feared fantasy for this issue: I would pretend to be him and he would pretend to be the neighbor. He was to be merciless in his criticism. Here is how it played out:

Client (As the neighbor):	"My yard looks much nicer than yours."
Me (As the client):	"You're right. You have a beautiful yard."
Client:	"My yard is a lot nicer. Your yard isn't good at all!"
Me:	"Right again, I just can't compete with your yard."
Client:	"Well, I have a hard time respecting someone who doesn't take better care of his yard."
Me:	"Well, your yard is beautiful and I can certainly tell that a nice-looking yard is important to you."
Client:	"I've talked to the neighbors and we all disrespect you for your yard."
Me:	"That's very interesting. There are certainly some high standards in this neighborhood. I have a lot of work to do to!"
Client:	"We so disrespect you because of your yard that we don't think you should live here anymore."
Me:	"Well, I would move, but no other neighborhood will have me!"

At that point, the client breaks out into laughter because he realizes how irrational his thinking has become. I asked him to imagine that a third person happened to overhear the conversation. What would that person think of him and the neighbor? Then we traded places and I played the neighbor and he played himself.

The key to this technique is that when you play the role of the client, you must not become defensive or argumentative about the criticism. You need to stay grounded and merely acknowledge and show empathy for the "critic's" comments. If you can think of nothing else, you can say things like "You have strong feelings about this." "That's very interesting to me. I never thought of that." "I'll have to take that under consideration."

Non-Defensive Responses to Criticism:　　This is another gem from *The Feeling Good Handbook*. Therapists can help clients be more courageous and assertive in social situations by giving them these tools to respond to criticism. You should explain to clients that the attitude underneath these techniques is more important than the techniques themselves. Their attitude needs to be "I will hear what you have to say and consider it, but it doesn't impact my feelings about myself." If clients can adopt that attitude, the techniques will come naturally. Here are the three techniques:

1. Empathy:　　Clients can be coached to show an understanding for the emotion behind the criticism without getting into its content. When I describe this to clients, I use myself as an example. Suppose a client says to me, "Hibbs, you are the sorriest excuse for a therapist I have ever seen. I think you are completely incompetent." Of course, that will be difficult to hear, but I would hope to keep my wits about me and say something like "You are really unhappy with me and disappointed in my work with you. This hasn't turned out like you hoped." You will note that I am not debating my skills as therapist. The real issue is that he is unhappy with my work and I need to acknowledge that.

2. Inquiry:　　This is simply inviting the critic to give you more information about the source of their unhappiness. This technique must be done with the proper attitude. You are not gathering ammunition for a counterargument. Instead, you convey a wish to truly understand that other person's point of view. So to my angry client I might say, "I want to understand your feelings, so please tell me what specific things I did that upset you."

3. Disarming:　　I love this technique. The goal here is to acknowledge whatever truth there may be in the criticism. No matter how unfair or unreasonable the criticism might be, there is usually an ounce of truth that we can find in there somewhere. So to my angry client I might reply, "I'm sure that I don't do everything perfectly and that I make mistakes."

Clients who are coached to use these techniques together will often feel empowered to deal with the critics in their lives. I once worked with a young married woman who was dreading an impending visit by her mother-in-law. My client had small children and a part-time job, so there wasn't much time for keeping the house clean and tidy. Her husband shared some of these duties with her, but he had a very challenging job, so his contributions were limited. Both of them accepted a less-than-immaculate house as a consequence of their busy lives. The mother-in-law, however, was very picky and often made snide comments about the condition of their home. Often she made these comments when the husband was not present. My client would become very upset during these visits.

In exploring her options, she decided to use the disarming technique. If the mother-in-law made a negative comment, she would agree with it. Yes, the house isn't as neat as it could be. Yes, she probably ought to be doing more. My client practiced this technique assiduously and felt well-prepared for the upcoming visit. However, when she returned to therapy three weeks later, she was very disappointed. Her mother-in-law had changed her ways and had no negative comments to make. Although my client was happy for this, she really wished she could have used the technique. These non-defensive responses to criticism are outlined in Handout 11-B.

No one likes to be criticized but it is impossible to go through life without getting negative feedback. Our initial response to criticism is almost always to defend, disagree, or mount a counterattack. This may feel like the right thing to do at the time, particularly if we feel that the criticism is unfair or unwarranted. However, a defensive response only leads to greater conflict and only encourages the other person to escalate their criticism. In his classic self-help book, *The Feeling Good Handbook*, Dr. David Burns describes three excellent alternatives to defensiveness.

Empathy: One excellent way to respond is to acknowledge and affirm the feeling behind the criticism without arguing about the content. So, if someone says, "You really messed things up this time," a good reply might be, "You're really unhappy with how I handled this." You might not think you "messed up," but that doesn't change the fact that the other person was unhappy with the outcome. You might as well acknowledge their feelings.

If someone says "You were so rude last night," a good reply might be, "I must have really hurt your feelings." Again, you might not think your behavior was "rude," but that isn't the point. The point is that the person was hurt by your actions.

Inquiry: A second response is to ask the other person to clarify or give more detail about what they are unhappy about. For example, "It would help me to know what I did that was rude." "What did I do that messed things up?" If you are going to use inquiry, it is important to have the right attitude. You are not asking for more information so you have ammunition to argue. ("That's no reason to be upset.") Instead, you need to be genuinely curious and interested in exactly what is bothering the other person.

Disarming: Even when criticism is grossly exaggerated or unfair, there is almost always an element of truth to the person's complaint. When you use disarming, you agree with whatever is true in the criticism, no matter how small. If someone says you were rude, you can reply with "I'm sure that I can be insensitive sometimes." If someone criticizes your work, you can reply with, "I'm sure that I sometimes make mistakes."

The attitude underneath these techniques is more important than the techniques themselves. Try to adopt an attitude of "I will listen to your criticism and respect your opinion. Nevertheless, your comments won't determine how I feel about myself."

Self-Disclosure: This is another technique that is deceptively simple but often difficult to apply. As already mentioned, socially anxious individuals are often very ashamed of their anxiety and go to great lengths to conceal it. Of course, this only makes the anxiety worse. As an alternative to hiding anxiety, the therapist can explore the possibilities that there may be some situations where it would be helpful for clients to disclose their anxiety. This is not an easy sell for clients and there may be some situations where they wouldn't want to use it. Nevertheless, there may be some situations in which it might be the perfect solution.

Let's go back to Bill whom we discussed some time ago. He was the IT/accountant who was asked to talk to his co-workers about the new accounting software. When the day came, Bill said to his colleagues, "Hey guys. I'm a geek, not a teacher or public speaker, so I'm not so comfortable explaining things. But, here it goes ..."

We can also recall Kenny who was asked to give the toast at his brother's wedding reception. He might begin with, "I can't believe my brother asked me to do this, because I'm really scared to do it. But since he asked me, here it goes ..."

When clients allow themselves to be open about their feelings, they often find that people are rooting for them and are not put off by the client's anxiety.

BEHAVIORAL PRACTICE

Once clients have been given the tools to manage social anxiety, they should be encouraged to gradually confront any social situations that they might have been avoiding. If they have turned down lunch invitations, they might try accepting them. If they have not gone to a professional meeting for a long time, they might try going to one, at least for a short time. They might even volunteer to make a short presentation to co-workers. Of course, this can seem very frightening, so therapists must maintain a patient and supportive attitude. You can ask the powerful question mentioned in Chapter Seven. ("When in the past did you do something that was very scary at first, but after a while it wasn't so bad?") Clients are more hopeful when they realize that they have already overcome fears in the past.

Clients can also develop courage by confronting their fears in small steps. The SUDS scale can be used to identify situations that are only mildly or moderately uncomfortable versus situations that engender extreme anxiety. Obviously, clients will want to tackle the easier situations first. Early exposure practice might include a supportive friend going with them. Then they can try to confront the situation by themselves.

At all times, client hesitation should be honored. Use Motivational Interviewing to help affirm the client's normal ambivalence. Once they have agreed to confront a particular situation between sessions, you can use the Motivational Ruler to strengthen the client's resolve to move forward. Handout 11-C can be used to help clients identify their goals.

In setting up behavioral goals for between session practice, it is important to make the client's goals behavioral and not emotional. Here is why: Gene has a PTA meeting tomorrow night. Before the meeting, people often mill about engaging in casual conversations. He finds this very uncomfortable because he doesn't know what to say. His typical approach is to wait until the meeting is about to begin and then slip in the back. He never engages in the meeting discussion and always slips out early to avoid having to talk with anyone. Perhaps his first goal would be to say, "Hi, how are you?" to one person. That's all. At his next session, his therapist asks him if he met his goal. He says that he did, but "I felt so anxious. I felt like the person could tell I was nervous. I felt stupid." You will notice that the client is expressing the ANT of "Discounting the positive." That is, he is not acknowledging the fact that he did what he said he would do. His therapist should say, "That's OK. The goal was not to feel a certain way. The goal was to do it. You did it, so we need to count it as a success. I promise you that if you keep practicing like this, eventually your feelings will catch up to your behavior."

What situations do you typically avoid (or if you cannot avoid them, they are extremely uncomfortable)?

What are your typical ANTS about these situations?

What strategies can you use to counter these ANTS (e.g., replacing them with more positive thoughts, mindfulness acceptance)?

What is your goal? What would you eventually want to be able to do?

What would be a small behavioral step in the direction of that goal?

Conversational Skills: If clients have been isolating themselves for a long time, they might not have developed effective conversational skills. Their ANTS might be "I don't know what to say to these people. We don't have anything in common. They are smarter/more educated/ more experienced/wealthier than I."

As mentioned earlier, the answer lies in changing your mission. Instead of trying to get other people to think highly of you, you encourage them to feel good about themselves. If you are willing to take this humble approach, I believe you can talk to anyone about almost anything. The secret is to be curious about the other person. Ask questions about them. The best questions are often open-ended questions, which tend to elicit more of response (e.g., instead of asking "Do you like your job?" you might ask "What do you like about your job?").

There are three topics that are usually safe to ask about. They spell the acronym FOR. F is for family. O is for occupation. R is for recreation. Easy examples are "Where are you from originally?" "Do you still have family back in Ohio?" "Do you have kids; how old are they?" "What kind of work do you do?" "How did you get into that career?" "I hear you're a football fan. What is your favorite team?" The next time you meet a new person, you might want to try this approach. See how long you can go before you have to say anything about yourself. If you have found someone who likes to talk about themselves, you might go a long time.

In preparing clients for social situations that will require conversation, you can coach them on how to apply FOR. If they know some of the other people, you can help them put together a list of FOR questions that they can have ready. If they do not know any of the people, you can help them create a generic list of questions. Thus prepared, clients are often surprised to see how easy it can be to carry on a conversation. Handout 11-D outlines these conversational tips for clients.

Handout 11-D
Simple Conversational Skills (FOR)

Do you avoid social situations because you are uncomfortable engaging in small talk? Perhaps your Automatic Negative Thoughts (ANTS) are "I have nothing in common with these people." Or, "I won't have anything to say and I'll make a fool of myself?"

However, the truth is that you can carry on a conversation with almost anyone if you are willing to change your mission (see Handout 11-A) and let go off any desire to impress the other person. You do not need to be intimidated by their knowledge, charms, or social status. All you need is to be polite and show genuine interest in them.

A good way to show interest in the other person is to be curious and ask questions. You can ask both closed-ended questions that can be answered in a word or two ("What kind of work do you do?") and open-ended questions that might require a longer response ("How do you like that kind of work?" "How do you like your new home?")

As far as content is concerned, there are three topics that are usually safe: family, occupation, and recreation. You can remember them with the simple acronym FOR.

"What kind of work do you do?"

"How did you get into that field?"

"Are you originally from this area?"

"What brought you here?"

"What do you do for fun?"

Avoid the impulse to compete with or outdo the other person. If the other person is excited because they are about to take their first overseas trip, don't deflate them by saying "Oh, I've traveled overseas a lot." Instead say, "What are you looking forward to the most?"

Also, don't feel intimated if the person talks about things that you can't relate to. For example, suppose I'm talking to someone who is excitedly talking about their recent trip to Italy. I might have the ANT "I've never been to Italy; I can't relate to them." If I go with this thought, I'll feel inadequate and uncomfortable. But what I should do is say, "I've never had the chance to go to Italy. What about it did you like the best?"

If you are willing to stay with this approach, you can carry on a lengthy conversation with almost anyone.

Think about any upcoming situation. Who will be there? What kind of FOR questions can you ask them?

Chapter Twelve:
Treating Generalized Anxiety Disorder

Generalized Anxiety Disorder (GAD) is the least clearly defined anxiety disorder. It is also often the most difficult to treat, possibly because it is sometimes co-morbid with depression, bipolar disorder, personality disorders, and substance abuse disorders.

The primary feature of GAD is excessive worry. Since everyone worries from time to time, it is difficult to determine what is "excessive." As a general rule, we call it GAD if the person tends to worry about a number of different situations. Anyone could go through a period in which they are worried about health, kids, finances, or career. However, in GAD the worry tends to transcend all issues so the person worries about almost everything, even issues well beyond their immediate life such as the economy in Europe or foreign terrorism.

An additional feature of GAD is that the worry occurs regularly and the individual finds it difficult to control. It seems to have taken over their lives.

Finally, to qualify for a diagnosis of GAD, the person must be experiencing at least three of the following symptoms:

1. Restlessness or feeling keyed up or on edge
2. Being easily fatigued
3. Difficulty concentrating or the mind going blank
4. Irritability
5. Muscle tension
6. Sleep disturbance (difficulty falling asleep or staying asleep, or restless unsatisfying sleep)

Many of these symptoms, such as restlessness, fatigue, irritability, muscle tension, and sleep disturbance, are indicative of high levels of physiological arousal. Therefore, our time-tested trio of interventions (deep breathing, relaxation, visualization) are all quite useful in the treatment of GAD. Progressive muscle relaxation is particularly helping in reducing muscle tension and promoting sound sleep.

The cognitive interventions for GAD have been thoroughly described in Chapter Six. Clients are asked to focus on a specific area of worry and write down their thoughts. The therapist, with permission, asks questions designed to gently challenge their thinking. All the while, the therapist is on the lookout for hidden assumptions, which will also be the focus of treatment.

From the perspective of Acceptance and Commitment Therapy (ACT), clients are encouraged to observe their worries with an attitude of kindness and compassion. Like all thoughts and feelings, worries are just mental events that come and go. We can take note of them and use them if they are helpful, or we can just let them pass by. Mindfulness meditation is designed to help develop this attitude of compassionate acceptance of our inner lives.

METACOGNITIVE THERAPY: UNHELPFUL BELIEFS ABOUT WORRY

Back in Chapter Two, I made brief mention of Metacognitive Therapy. This approach has been described by Adrian Wells in his book *Metacognitive Therapy for Anxiety and Depression*. In Metacognitive Therapy the focus is not on the content of our thoughts. Instead the focus is on what we believe about our thoughts. Dr. Wells and his colleagues have identified several metacognitive beliefs about worry, which tend to make worry worse.

Worry is terribly harmful: Often you will hear clients say things like "I know this worry will kill me." "I'm going to worry myself to death." "This worry is going to drive me crazy." "I'm going to end up like my mother who was hospitalized when she was 60."

These comments suggest clients are afraid that they are causing themselves grave physical or mental harm by worrying. That is, they are excessively worried about their worry. Metacognitive therapists refer to this as "level 2 worry."

When clients verbalize these thoughts, it is helpful to discuss this with them. What type of damage do they think they are causing? Where did they get the idea that worry is so dangerous? After this discussion, therapists can reassure clients that worry is normal and that almost everyone, including exceptional healthy individuals, worries from time to time.

It's not that we want people to worry. We just don't want them to worry so much about their worry.

Worry is helpful or necessary: Perhaps you have heard comments like "Worry helps me prepare for the worst." "Worry makes me work harder." "I'm afraid not to worry, because then the bad thing might happen." "Maybe worry will help me find a solution."

These statements suggest a need to hold on to worry because it is believed to serve an important function. Often there is some element of truth to these beliefs. Yes, worry can motivate. Yes, worry can help you look for solutions. However, often these same benefits can be achieved without excessive worry. In exploring this issue with clients, the powerful question to ask is "Is there a way to achieve the same benefit without so much worry?"

I was working with a gentleman who had moved to Atlanta about a year ago to begin a new job. He had been on this job for almost a year, and from all accounts he seemed to be doing OK. However, his manager had a negative approach and it was difficult to get positive feedback from him. Because of this, my client was constantly worried about losing his job. Even though the worry was interfering with his quality of life, he was reluctant to give it up because "I'll be prepared if I lose my job." I asked if there might be a way to prepare for job loss without the extreme worry. We explored this together and he came up with a good contingency plan. If he were to lose his job, he would move back to his hometown in Arizona and live with family members until he could get back on his feet. Even though he didn't want that to happen, he at least realized that he would not be on the street. With that, his worry was greatly reduced.

Worry cannot be controlled: Certainly worry feels uncontrollable at times, but is it really? I think we do have at least some capacity to limit our worry. Even though ANTS are uncontrollable, the process of worry requires us to dwell on the ANTS and take them too seriously.

To help clients feel more in control of their worry, you can look for situations in which the worry was naturally interrupted. For example, a woman said to me, "I worried all weekend. It was terrible." I asked her to think through the weekend to see if there were any times when the worry stopped or at least was greatly reduced. She mentioned that her sister had called her Sunday afternoon and they had had a nice talk. During the phone call, she was not focused on the source of her worry so she felt much better. However, as soon as the call ended, the worry was back in full force. This gave us some idea of how we might give her some relief from her worry. Perhaps she could plan to have more phone conversations with her sister. Perhaps there were other friends she could contact. Since she was going through a difficult time, perhaps she could stay with her sister for a while. This discussion did not make everything better, but it did give her some relief and helped her feel more in control of her worry.

It is helpful to have a discussion about these common beliefs about worry. Handout 12-A can be used to facilitate the discussion.

HANDOUT 12-A
FAULTY BELIEFS ABOUT WORRY

Everyone worries at one time or other. If worry weren't bad enough, many of us have certain beliefs about worry that make the problem worse than it needs to be. Three common beliefs about worry are listed below. Without knowing it, many of us hold some of these beliefs. Do you recognize any of these beliefs in yourself?

1. Worry is terribly harmful: Do you worry about how much you worry? Do you find yourself thinking or even saying things like "I'm going to worry myself to death!" "If I don't stop worrying like this, I know I'll go crazy." "My mother had a 'nervous breakdown' when she was 55 years old. If I don't get better control of my worry, I'm going to end up like her." As you can imagine, thoughts like these only serve to make worry worse.

It's not that worrying is a good thing. Your therapist is going to teach you skills to help you worry less. In the meantime, maybe you can give yourself a break by internalizing the following facts:

a. Everyone worries sometimes.
b. Worry and anxiety will not make you go crazy or psychotic.
c. There are numerous people who worry a lot but are still in great physical condition.
d. The body is resilient and is quite capable of rebounding from stress.
e. Even the biggest worrier can learn how to worry less.

2. Worry is helpful or necessary: Sometimes we hold on to worry because we believe worry serves a purpose. Do you find yourself saying things like "Do I need to worry about this?" "At what point do you think I should start worrying about this?"

We hold on to worry for several reasons. First, sometimes we have the superstitious belief that worry itself will keep the bad thing from happening. Second, sometimes we feel that worry will help us prepare for the bad result. Third, sometimes we think worry will help us find solutions to the problem.

If you are prone to this belief, ask yourself, "Is there a way to get the same benefit without so much worry?" "Can I look for solutions for the problem without so much worry?" "Can I prepare myself for a bad outcome without so much worry?" "Is there any harm in my having a positive attitude for now and then dealing with the bad outcome if and when it comes?"

3. Worry cannot be controlled: There are certainly times when worry feels uncontrollable. The more we try not to think about the distressing situation, the more the worry haunts us. However, we might be able to control worry better than we think.

But first we have to make a distinction between ANTS and worry. Since ANTS are, by definition, "automatic," we do not have any control over them. We don't go searching for them; they just pop into our heads. And any effort to not have the ANT will likely cause it to hang around longer.

What we can control, however, is how we interpret the ANT and how much credence we give to it. If we can see it as "just a thought" and let it pass, we will be fine. But if we dwell on the ANT and see it as "the truth," then our worry can spin out of control

To gain better control over your worry, take note of situations when it was interrupted naturally. Maybe you worried most of the weekend, but you felt much better during a 90-minute phone conversation with your sister. Maybe you noticed some easing of the worry when you did some volunteer work at your church.

If these activities gave you at least some temporary relief, how can you use this information to help you worry less? Should you call your sister or other loved ones more often? Would it help you to increase your volunteer work at the church?

CIRCLE OF INFLUENCE VS. CIRCLE OF CONCERN

When we get to this section of my seminar I ask my attendees to pay close attention. If they get nothing else from the presentation, I want them to get this idea. This is something that I discuss with clients several times a day, and they tell me that it is one of the most important things they learned in therapy.

Many of our difficulties are created by our tendency to focus on things that we cannot control while neglecting things that we can control. Much of our effectiveness depends on our ability to discern when we have control and when we do not. To help clients have a nice way to visualize this idea, I talk with them about the Circle of Influence vs. the Circle of Concern. I first learned about these circles while reading *The Seven Habits of Highly Effective People* by the late Dr. Stephen R. Covey. A client-friendly description of these circles is offered in Handout 12-B.

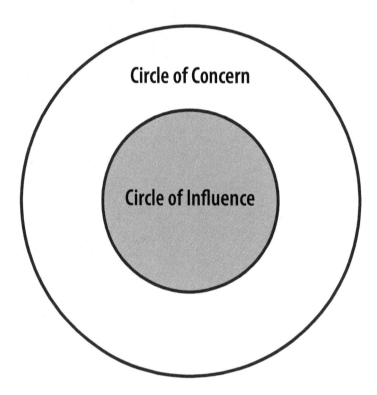

The Circle of Influence consists of those things over which we have control. Basically this involves our own behavior and attitudes and little else. The Circle of Concern consists of those things over which we have no control. This includes the thoughts, feelings, and behaviors of others. It also includes the societal forces that impact our lives such as the economy, political systems, and the community in which we were born. It also includes natural phenomena such as the weather or the occurrence of natural disasters. The Circle of Concern also includes our basic genetic endowment. Finally, it even includes our past, because we cannot change anything that happened before this moment. We can change our response to that event, but we cannot change the fact that it happened.

It is a fundamental principle of life that we are the most effective when we focus on the inner circle, the Circle of Influence. When we do this, we become empowered and our Circle of Influence tends to expands. We have an increased capacity to influence the outcome of any situation.

We are the least effective when we focus on the outer circle, the Circle of Concern. When we do this, we become disempowered and have less influence over our circumstances.

For example, a client might say to me, "I can't get a job because I am 55 years old and the economy is poor." Even though those factors directly impact his employability, they are things that he cannot control. If this is his focus, what will his job search be like? He is likely to feel defeated before he begins and his job search might lack direction or enthusiasm. On the other hand, he may say to himself, "What do I need to do to get a job? I can consult with a job coach or get more training. I can do power networking in which I ask my friends to ask their friends about job openings. I can post my resume on all the job sites and contract recruiters. I set a goal to contact 5–10 potential employers per day." Obviously, his job search is much more likely to be effective.

It is interesting to note where our thoughts go and how easy it is to drift out into the Circle of Concern while neglecting the Circle of Influence. A woman might tell me, "I have been upset all week. All I can think about is how much happier my ex-husband is with his new wife. The thought of that just kills me!" Of course, I am going to show empathy for her feelings, but at some point I am going to gently ask her what circle she is in. Clearly, she is focusing on something she cannot control. Then I might ask her what would be in the inner circle. She might have great difficulty identifying this at first. Eventually, she might begin to cry and talk about things she could be doing to adjust to her divorce, but she is not doing them. She could get a new job or start doing volunteer work. She could travel. She could accept more social invitations. She could get involved with some activity like joining the church, going to book club, or going back to Weight Watchers. These are all things that she can control so she will do well to focus on them.

During our discussion of social anxiety, I explained that socially anxious individuals are "mind reading." They are focusing on the thoughts of other people, which is something they clearly cannot control. However, if they change their mission and say to themselves, "I will be polite and treat people with respect," their anxiety will decrease and they will have better social interactions.

Dr. Covey refers to the Circle of Concern as the circle of "have." "I wish I had a better job." "I wish I had more money." "I wish that people treated me better." The Circle of Influence is referred to as the circle of "be." "What kind of person do I need to be in this situation?" "How can I do a better job?"

People who live primarily in the Circle of Concern will not take responsibility for their lives. They feel victimized by people and circumstances that they cannot control. People who focus on the Circle of Influence assume responsibility for their lives. They are constantly asking themselves what they can do about any situation. If they cannot change the situation, they can always change their attitude about the situation.

Here is another illustration. I am sure that you have had clients who say things like "Things are not fair at my job. This guy comes in late all the time and never gets into trouble. This woman leaves early and never gets in trouble. They all gossip, do sloppy work, but the boss never gets on them. But, if I dare ask to leave early, the boss says I can't." Again, I would show empathy for the client's feelings, but she is focusing on things she cannot control. She cannot control what her colleagues do or how her boss treats them. She cannot change the "fairness" of her boss' behavior. However, she can control what time she gets to work, the time she leaves, how well she does her job, whether or not she gossips, and how well she communicates with her boss and co-workers. If she puts her focus on this, she will feel better and will be more effective on the job.

Here is a final example. When I work with couples, I usually draw these circles in one of our first few sessions. People come to marital therapy to change the behavior of their spouse, but the spouse's behavior is in the outer circle. They cannot change it. The behavior changes they want in their spouse may be absolutely reasonable and appropriate. But the way they try to get these changes (e.g., complaining, criticism, put downs, whining) might actually be working against them.

As an alternative, I encourage clients to focus on what they can do to improve their marriage. Can they be more thoughtful? Can they be a better listener? Can they express their desires in a respectful manner? If the husband and wife can both focus on what they can do to make this better, we have a much greater chance of making progress.

Early in my career, I worked in the addiction field and I had the opportunity to attend 12-step meetings such as AA, NA, and Al-Anon. Quite often, the meeting will open and close with the following prayer, originally written by the theologian Reinhold Niebuhr.

"God grant me the serenity to accept the things that I cannot change; the courage to change the things that I can; and the wisdom to know the difference."

Those 12-step people, in their great wisdom, have long ago discovered the principles exemplified in Dr. Covey's circles.

Often we are paralyzed by worry because we are focusing on things we cannot control and not attending to things we can control. Much of our emotional well-being depends on our being able to clearly see the difference between what we can and cannot control. A powerful way to visualize this was described by the late Dr. Stephen Covey in his classic book, *The Seven Habits of Highly Effective People*.

Imagine two concentric circles. Dr. Covey referred to the inner circle as the Circle of Influence. This consists of those things in life that we can change by our own will. In general, this consists of our own behavior, our attitude, and not much else. The outer circle is called the Circle of Concern and consists of all the many things that affect us but over which we have no control. This includes the thoughts, feelings, and behavior of other people. It also includes external factors like the weather or state of the economy. Finally, it includes the past because it cannot be changed. However, we can change how we think about and deal with past events in the here and now.

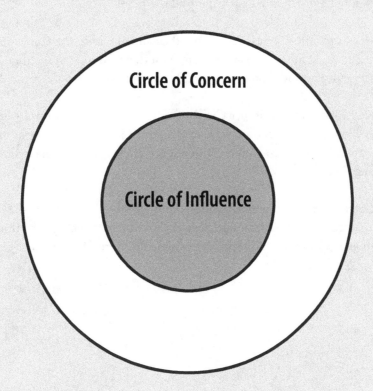

It is a basic principle in life that we are more effective (and worry less) when we focus on the Circle of Influence. When we do that, we become empowered and the Circle of Influence grows. That is, we end up having more influence over a situation than we previously had. We are less effective (and worry more) when we focus on the outer circle. When we do this, we become disempowered and our Circle of Influence shrinks.

Here is an example. I am working with an unemployed client who tells me "I can't get a job because I'm 55 years old. They're just not hiring people my age in this recession." I cannot deny that these factors might impact his ability to find work. But look where his focus is. He cannot change his age or the economy, so they clearly are in the outer Circle of Concern. So if these two factors are the center of his thinking, what will his job search be like? There is a good chance that he will be defeated before he even starts.

Now let's imagine that this unemployed gentleman decided to focus on the inner Circle of Influence. Likely his thinking would be, "What do I need to do to find work? Should I consult with a vocational counselor or job coach? Do I need to get some more training? Maybe I should do some power networking by telling my friends to tell their friends. Maybe I should contact a few recruiters or post my resume on as many job search websites as possible. Maybe I should set a goal of directly contacting ten potential employers every day." Clearly, his job search is more likely to be successful.

It is very easy to drift out into the Circle of Concern; in fact, it can be quite comfortable. However, we don't get very far when we do this.

I worked with a client who was constantly frustrated with the management and co-workers at her place of employment. She would say things like "That guy comes in late all the time and he never gets into trouble. That woman leaves early and she never gets into trouble. But if I take a little extra time for lunch, I get called on the carpet. Besides, my co-workers are lazy and are gossiping all the time."

Her complaints were legitimate, but it is easy to see that they all fall within the Circle on Concern. She cannot control what her co-workers do or how her manager deals with them. As long as she thinks this way, she will feel like a victim and have a negative attitude about her work. It might even negatively impact her work performance.

I asked her to think about what might be in her Circle of Influence. Can she control when she arrives to work, when she leaves, and how long she takes for lunch? Can she do her job to the best of her ability? Can she have a positive attitude on the job and treat her co-workers with respect? If she has some concerns to voice to her manager, can she express her feelings in a positive way?

If you ever attended 12-Step meetings such as AA and Al-Anon, they will often recite the following prayer: "God grant me the serenity to accept the things I cannot change; the courage to change the things that I can; and the wisdom to know the difference." This powerful prayer perfectly illustrates the Circles of Influence and Concern.

DALE CARNEGIE'S THREE-STEP WORRY TECHNIQUE

Dale Carnegie was not a psychologist; he was a salesman and motivational writer. His classic book, *How to Win Friends and Influence People,* is still one of the best-selling self-help books of all time. Not everyone knows that Mr. Carnegie wrote another book entitled *How to Stop Worrying and Start Living.* This book contains a lot of great folksy wisdom.

One of my favorite ideas in the book is his simple three-step process for dealing with worry. This is an idea that you can use for yourself and you can use it as a tool to help a client struggling with worry. You don't need to have an anxiety disorder to benefit from this process. You just need to be worried about something.

Here are the three steps. First, you imagine the worst case scenario. What is absolutely the worst thing that could happen in this situation? Clients will often be reluctant to consider the worst case. They will say things like "I can't think about that." "It upsets me too much to think about that." "I'm afraid that thinking about it will make it happen." As always, therapists need to be empathetic to the client's feeling, however you might point out that they are thinking about it already. Otherwise, they wouldn't be worrying. You might suggest that it might be helpful to get the worst case on the table.

The second step is even harder. Now that the worst case is on the table, emotionally accept that it might possibly happen. You don't want it to happen and you are not resigned to it. You are going to do what you reasonably can to prevent it. Nevertheless, if it happens, it happens, and you will deal with it if it does.

To help clients with this difficult second step of acceptance, you can ask the following three questions: (1) What would be the real consequences should the worst thing happen? (2) How would you cope with those consequences should they happen? (3) What would still be good in your life?

The third step is to take whatever practical steps you can to prevent the worst case and improve your outcome.

I first learned of this technique many years ago when I was a callow undergraduate student. There was one term when I was seriously behind in my school work. I had midterm exams to study for and papers to begin. (You know the feeling!) To cope with my intense anxiety, I applied this technique.

First, I actually computed my worst-possible grade point average for the term. It was pretty bad, but that was the worst it could be.

Second, I emotionally accepted the worst-case scenario. I asked myself the three important questions: (1) What would be the real consequences? (Academic probation and angry parents.) (2) How would I cope with those consequences? (I would return to the behavior of previous terms in which I had done quite well. I would apologize to my parents and suggest that I might do better if I left the car at home next term.) (3) What would still be good in my life? (Actually, quite a lot! I will still have my friends, family, health, music, and the beauty of nature.)

Third, I worked to prevent the worst-case scenario. Now that I was reasonably calm, I was able to focus and get to work, and my final grades were much higher than my worst case.

There will no doubt be situations in which clients are facing a situation that is so horrendous and terrifying that this technique might not be helpful. There may be consequences that they cannot accept no matter how hard they try. However, I have personally used this technique at some very challenging times, including once when I was desperately concerned about the health of one of my children. I can't say that this technique made everything better, but it did help me gain some perspective on the issue and find some good solutions. This Three-Step Process is described for clients in Handout 12-C.

HANDOUT 12-C
DALE CARNEGIE'S THREE-STEP PROCESS FOR WORRY

Many people are familiar with the classic self-help book *How to Win Friends and Influence People* by Dale Carnegie. But you might not know that Mr. Carnegie wrote another book called *How to Stop Worry and Start Living*. Mr. Carnegie was not a mental health professional but his book contains a lot of folksy wisdom. One of the best techniques from his book is his simple three-step process for handling worry. The three steps are as follows:

1. Imagine the worst possible outcome to your current concern. Many are reluctant to do this because it upsets them too much. "I don't want to think about it; it scares me too much." The problem is that they are already thinking about it; that's why they're worried. So let's go ahead and get it out on the table.

2. Emotionally accept that the worst-case scenario might actually happen. You are not resigning yourself to it, but you can at least consider the possibility that it will happen. To help you with this acceptance, you can ask yourself these three questions: (1) What will be the real consequences if the bad thing happens? (2) How will I cope with those consequences?(3) What will still be good in my life?

3. Now that you have accepted the worst-case scenario, do what you reasonably can to prevent it. Take practical steps to get a better outcome.

I learned this model as an undergraduate student. One term I was way behind in my work and I was very anxious about my grades. So, I decided to try this model.

First step: I actually calculated my worst possible grade point average. It was pretty bad!

Second step: I worked to accept the worst case by asking myself the three questions. What would be the real consequences? It would likely mean academic probation and upset parents. How would I cope with those consequences? I had done well before, so I would just need to return to my former good study habits. As far as my parents were concerned, I would beg their forgiveness. What would still be good in my life? Actually, there was a lot that would be good. I still had college for now. My parents would not disown me. I would still have my friends, my health, and many other good things.

Third step: Once I used steps one and two to calm down a bit, I got to work. As is often the case with things we worry about, my grades were much better than I feared.

THE DVD MODEL FOR INTRUSIVE WORRY

There are times when we are wrestling with a situation that so overwhelms us that we find it difficult to think of anything except the source of the worry. To help clients with this kind of worry, I often present the DVD Model. I ask the client to imagine that a DVD disk corresponds to the entire content of their mind, memories, language—anything they could imagine. I then tell them that the TV screen or monitor represents what happens to be in their conscious awareness at any point in time. Obviously, there is a huge amount of information on the disk and relatively less on the screen. I might say to the client, "You're probably not thinking of the name of your high school, but ..." Immediately the name of their high school pops into their mind.

If something comes on the screen that upsets us, our impulse is to say to ourselves, "Stop thinking about that!" Unfortunately, trying not to think about something usually causes the thought to remain in our awareness. You might think of it as pushing the pause button on your remote control. When you do that, the image just remains in your mind.

Using the analogy of the DVD player and remote control, I share four alternative methods for dealing with intrusive worry. I lay these four options out as a menu and ask if they would like to try one or two of them. Usually they do. Here are the four alternatives:

1. Change the channel: This means simply creating a menu of pleasant memories, relaxing scenes, or affirming or inspirational thoughts. Then when clients feel overwhelmed by the upsetting thought, they can just pick up the remote control and change the channel. Of course, they might go back to the upsetting thought, but this tool can help them get some relief.

2. Fast forward and rewind: Rather than trying to stop having the upsetting thought, clients are coached to have the thought on purpose, but to run through it quickly and let it play out to its end. For example, someone plagued with financial worries might decide to imagine all the possible negative outcomes. They lose their job, their home, their family, etc. As soon as they have thought through the negative outcome, they back up and think it again. It is like watching a scary movie for the 20th time. It just isn't scary anymore. Often clients will find that when they purposely think the bad thought, the mind will eventually let it go. In the treatment of obsessive-compulsive disorder, this technique is called "imaginal exposure," in which the clients think about their obsession on purpose.

3. Record for future viewing: This involves clients deciding to have a specific time to think about the upsetting situation. If they notice themselves obsessing about the problem at a different time, they will remind themselves that this is not the time. They will then immediately focus on something pleasant, productive, or both. They can thus delay the worry until the designated time. Of course, when the time comes, they might not be inclined to worry about it, but at least they will have the chance if they want.

4. Comedy channel: This is a helpful technique for negative thoughts that are self-critical or threatening. Clients are encouraged to imagine that these negative thoughts are being spoken by someone for whom they have no respect; someone who is ridiculous and whose opinion is not worth considering. Often clients choose fictional characters such as Homer Simpson or Archie Bunker. I recently had a client with severe OCD. When he began to have troublesome obsessions, he would imagine them in the voice of Donald Duck. If clients cannot think of a character, you can help them make one up. Good examples might be

"Mr. Negative," "The Critic," or "The Party Pooper." The idea is to help clients not take their negative thoughts so seriously.

Again, how you present this technique is important. Do not present each of them separately. Instead, lay them out as a menu of options. I usually say, "Here are four techniques that some people find helpful. I will describe each of them and then you can decide if you would like to try one or two of them." When presented this way, clients will often choose at least one technique and find that it gives them some relief. Use Handout 12-D to present these techniques to clients.

HANDOUT 12-D
THE DVD MODEL FOR INTRUSIVE WORRY

Sometimes there are issues that are so troubling that we almost cannot think of anything else. It is like the ANTS have taken over and we feel powerless to do anything about them. If you are struggling with this kind of intrusive, obsessive worry, here are some techniques that might give you some relief.

These techniques are all based on the model of a DVD player. Imagine that a DVD disk corresponds to the entire contents of you mind—all your memories, imagination, language, everything. The TV screen or monitor corresponds to what happens to be in your conscious awareness at any point in time. Obviously, the disk contains a lot more than the screen, and the content of the screen is constantly changing.

When some thought or image comes up on the screen that distresses us, our natural tendency is to resist it. We might even say to ourselves, "Stop thinking about that." Unfortunately, we now understand that ANTS are automatic and trying "not" to think them usually backfires. In fact, trying "not" to think something is like pushing the pause button on your DVD. The distressing thought or image just stays there on the screen.

However, using this analogy of a DVD player, there are four other strategies that you can try. Many people find one or more of these helpful in reducing the intensity of the worry.

Change the channel: If what comes up on the screen is too distressing, one thing you can do is pick up the remote control and simply change the channel. In other words, you can create a menu of thoughts, images, and memories that you can switch to whenever you feel the need. It could be a pleasant memory or an image of a place where you feel safe and comfortable. If might be a favorite prayer, scriptural verse, poem, affirmation, or inspirational saying. It might involve thinking of someone who is very dear to you. It's not that you're resisting the negative thought. You are just choosing to give yourself a break and focus on something more positive.

Fast forward and rewind: Rather than resisting the unpleasant thought or image, go ahead and think it on purpose. But run through it quickly. Allow your mind to go all the way to the worst-case scenario. Then back up and run it again. I once worked with a man who was afraid of losing his job, his home, and his marriage. I encouraged him to let his mind quickly visualize all the disasters and then go back and visualize them again. He did this over and over until eventually he become bored with it.

Record for future viewing: Another tactic is to designate a specific place and time when you will decide to purposely think about the worrisome situation. If you find yourself worrying about it at some other time, just say to yourself, "This isn't the time for this. I'll think about this tonight at 7:30." Then immediately replace the worry with something pleasant, productive, or both.

Comedy channel: This is a good technique when the negative thought is self-critical or threatening. What you can do is imagine that these negative thoughts are being spoken to you by someone for whom you have no regard or respect at all. It might be a real person or a fictional person such as Homer Simpson or Archie Bunker. One client with severe OCD imagined that his obsessions were being spoken by Donald Duck. Or perhaps you would like to give your negative thoughts a name such as "Mr. Negative, "The Critic," or "Party Pooper."

BEHAVIORAL INTERVENTIONS FOR WORRY

Consistent with the Three C's model of anxiety, we always encourage clients to gradually resist their urge to avoid anxiety-arousing situations and start confronting them. With the other anxiety disorders, it is clear what the behavior is. The individual with panic attacks need to confront situations that have triggered panic. Socially anxious people need to start doing social things. People afraid to drive on highways or fly in airplanes need to do the things they fear.

But when it comes to worry, what is the behavior? What is the client avoiding? Actually the behavior that is being avoided is doing something about the problem at hand. Much of the procrastination in this world is caused by anxiety. A person starts thinking about a problem but feels so frightened and overwhelmed by it that he immediately puts it aside.

You have no doubt seen clients who are deathly afraid of medical problems. However, they have not been to a doctor in years, because they are afraid of what the doctor is going to tell them. Likewise, people who are worried about financial concerns have not made a budget or even looked at their checkbook. Again, they are avoiding the issue out of fear.

I have worked with students who were working on their doctoral dissertations. One woman told me that she had not spoken to her major professor in four months. Why? Because she was afraid that he was angry at her for not calling him for four months! And so the problem continues.

Once you have given clients the physiological and cognitive tools to manage their excessive anxiety, your next step is to help them take action. You might think of moving away from your role as a therapist and moving into the role of a life coach.

It is at this point that you will want to ask the powerful question, "What is one specific thing, no matter how small, that you can do to address this problem? What is something you can do right now?" It does not matter how small the step is, as long it is in the direction that they client wants to go. If might be as small as:

"Make a list of possible options."

"Call my father and ask his advice."

"Make an appointment with the doctor."

"Write out a pro and con list for this important decision."

"Look at my bank statement."

"Ask four people for their opinion."

"Call my son's teacher."

"Update my resume."

"Download and read two articles about my illness."

"Start checking my blood sugar."

"Find out where the AA meetings are."

Clients should be encouraged to set a specific timetable for this action; the sooner the better. Then you can gently raise the issue of accountability. Would they be willing to let you know when they have completed the task? Could they send you an email or leave a voice mail message? Every evening, I receive emails that say things like "Studied for my exam as planned."

"Talked to my wife about our budget." "Attended my first AA meeting." Clients like having this way to check in with me, and it sends the message that I care about their progress.

In some situations, there might not be any specific thing that can be done immediately, but there might be something that could be done at a specified time in the future. Perhaps they are waiting for the most recent financial statement from their business. Perhaps they are waiting on a medical report. Maybe they are waiting for the testing results for their child who is struggling in school. In these situations, clients can make a commitment to take some definitive action once they have the information they need.

Once these first steps have been taken, you can help the client map out any additional steps that need to be taken with a definite timetable for the completion of each step. The client will then have a clear path to deal with the problem at hand. Often their inactivity has only added to their worry. Once they start taking productive steps, their worry will decrease significantly. My mantra is, "The best way to reduce worry is to take action!"

During this phase of treatment, the focus should shift away from feelings and toward behavior. Not "How are you feeling" but instead "What are you doing?" If I have a long history and excellent rapport with a client, I have even been so bold as to say, "We have been talking about your feelings a lot. From now on, I want to talk about your feelings as little as possible and focus on what you are doing."

I recently worked with a 53-year-old sales executive who was totally stressed out by his job. He was working too many hours, losing sleep, but still not quite making his sales numbers. He hated his job but stayed on because he doubted that he could find a comparable job as his age. His situation so upset him that he could not look for solutions. Instead, he numbed himself by having a few glasses of wine every evening.

After we had employed the standard physiological and cognitive interventions, he needed to take action on two different fronts. He needed to increase his productivity at work, while looking for other job opportunities. His first two action steps were: (1) Make an appointment with his manager to get an accurate assessment of what the manger's expectations were. (2) Start updating his resume. He set specific deadlines to complete these tasks and agreed to check in with me regularly on his progress. Even these two little steps helped to decrease his anxiety significantly.

Of course the timing of this intervention is crucial. If you explore action steps without first giving the client the necessary physiological and cognitive tools, they will balk at taking action. Motivational Interviewing is a wonderful tool to explore clients' ambivalence about change and knowing when to encourage specific actions steps. Handout 12-E can be used to help clients identify appropriate action steps.

The best cure for anxiety is to take action! We can be so overwhelmed with anxiety that we are not taking practical steps to address the source of our concern. We worry about our health, but don't make a doctor's appointment. We fret about our finances, but don't make a budget or even balance our checkbook. We wonder about a relationship, but we avoid having a conversation that might make things better.

You have learned techniques to calm the body such as deep breathing relaxation and visualization. We have learned how to correct our thinking by identifying our ANTS and learning more productive ways to manage and interpret them.

Now, it is time for the third step, confront your fears. With the help of your therapist, friend, and/or relative, begin to generate possible solutions to your problem. Maybe you see no possible solutions but it's likely that someone else will see what you cannot see at this time. To help you take action, here are some questions to ask yourself.

What is one specific thing I can do immediately to begin to address this problem?

When will I take this action and to whom will I be accountable to get it done?

What additional information do I need to address this problem? How will I get it?

If there is nothing I can do about the problem right now, what is something I could do at a specified time in the future?

Who can help me consider alternative ways to think about and address this problem?

Chapter Thirteen: A Final Note from the Dapper Gentleman in Pittsburgh

I hope that you have caught some of the passion that I feel about helping people overcome anxiety problems. I must admit that I am somewhat of a zealot on this matter. With what we know today, there is no need for anyone to be overcome with anxiety. There is no need to let anxiety keep anyone from living life to its fullest.

I want to leave you with a final note, something I relearned while conducting a seminar in Pittsburgh. One of my attendees was a delightful gentleman who looked like he might have been in his 70s or 80s. I gathered that he was at least that old when he mentioned that he had received his training in the 1940s and early 50s. He was impeccably dressed in a light gray suit and spoke in a very urbane European (Austrian perhaps?) accent. He paid close attention throughout the program and asked several very cogent questions.

As I was bringing the program to a close, he raised his hand to make one final comment. He said, "I have learned a lot today and I am excited to start applying much of what you have shared with us. However, I have one concern. Much of what you have covered today has focused on techniques. They are wonderful, but if we focus too much on technique, we will forget the importance of the relationship. The research on psychotherapy has consistently shown that it is the therapist-patient relationship that is the most important."

My immediate response was to agree with him completely and thank him for reminding me of such an important truth. He was so right! The classic early research on psychotherapy conducted by Carl Rogers and others is still relevant. The ability to show empathy, genuineness, and unconditional positive regard are still the key elements of an effective therapist-client relationship. I pass on this gentleman's thoughtful reminder to you.

Suggested Reading

Burns, David, *The Feeling Good Handbook*. New York 1989.

Carnegie, Dale, *How to Stop Worrying and Start Living*. New York, Pocket Books, 2004.

Chansky, Tamar, *Freeing Yourself from Anxiety: Four Simple Steps to Overcome Worry and Create the Life You Want,* Cambridge, MA, Da Capo Press, 2012.

Clark, David & Beck, Aaron, *Cognitive Therapy of Anxiety Disorders.* New York, Guilford Press, 2010.

Covey, Stephen R., *The Seven Habits of Highly Effective People.* New York, Simon & Schuster, 2004.

Forsyth, John & Eifert, Georg, *The Mindfulness & Acceptance Workbook for Anxiety,* Oakland, CA, New Harbinger Publications, 2007.

Hibbs, Stanley, *Anxiety Gone: The Three C's of Anxiety Recovery,* Mustang, OK, Dare2Dream Books, 2007.

Miller, William R. & Rollnick, Rollnick, Stephen, *Motivational Interviewing: Preparing People for Change,* New York, Guilford Press, 2004.

Wells, Adrian, Metacognitive Therapy for Anxiety and Depression, New York, Guilford Press, 2009.